Contents

Chapter 1

Series Introduction

Kate Ashcroft

The research that colleges and universities engage in covers a very wide spectrum, including basic research into fundamental problems as well as entrepreneurial work, often contracted by a particular customer. Each of the books in this series is focused on a particular form of research: that of small-scale insider research. Each looks at issues of teaching, learning and management within colleges and universities. The aim is to provide you with starting points for research that will improve your practice, that of your students and the context for learning and teaching that your institution provides. The research that you undertake may also help you to understand the context in which teaching and learning is managed and should provide you with the raw material for publication in research-based media.

The series is aimed at creating a range of quick and easy to read handbooks, so you can get started on research into aspects of your practice. Each book includes a version of this introductory chapter by the series editor about insider research, its principles and methods.

The chapters in this book are focused on contemporary issues relating to assessment and evaluation. They include a range of examples of research instruments and suggestions as to how you might use or adapt them to your own context for enquiry. The starting points for research cover the following areas:

- the perspectives of the main participants in the business of assessment and evaluation;
- the context in which they operate;
- their existing practice;
- their existing values; and
- the relationships between the context and the values and practice.

A range of methods used in insider research into assessment and evaluation is included within the research tasks.

None of the books includes sufficient information for you to complete a research project for publication. You will need to find out more about the particular aspects of assessment or evaluation and the research methodology that you decide to use. Similarly, the book will introduce you to some of the theoretical frameworks open to you, but the discussion will not be deep enough, of itself, to ensure that your research is grounded in theory. For these reasons, an annotated reading list is included at the end of each chapter.

Synopsis of the Series

The series is designed to appeal to lecturers in further and higher education who are interested in developing research skills and who would find concrete suggestions for research and some exemplar research questions and instruments helpful. We have tried to avoid using technical terms and jargon unnecessarily, but where these have to be included, we have tried to explain them in as simple a way as possible.

Increasingly, lecturers are required to produce regular research papers. In the UK, the process of research rating means that lecturers in universities restrict their career opportunities if they do not engage regularly in research and publication. (I describe the process of research rating in the introductory chapter to Bennett *et al.*, 1996.) Many do not know where to start. Others are unable to manage their time in order to incorporate their research and publication alongside their teaching work. Some feel that a commitment to research would detract from their preferred role as teachers.

The series provides a framework of ideas and starting points for research which can be carried out alongside your current practice. The books present these ideas in such a way that, rather than detracting from your practice, they might enhance it. They introduce methods for you to use (adapted or unadapted) for researching into your own teaching. For example, a description of the process of action research is included in Chapter 6. This process is applicable to a variety of research problems.

You should find the books useful if you are new to teaching or if you are an experienced lecturer who needs or wishes to develop a research and publication profile within education. In the case of higher education, this is a major focus that involves all tutors. You may be under pressure to publish for the first time in order to contribute to research rating exercises. You might be undertaking a qualification that includes a research element. A masters degree or doctorate is an increasing requirement for promotion in further and higher education. In the UK, more masters degree courses are being developed and geared towards this sector. In higher education, many staff are now expected to achieve a doctorate. Some of the starting points within this book could be developed into a fairly sophisticated research project.

You may be interested in researching your own practice for its own sake. For instance, you may wish to explore your students' actions in response to various assessment tasks that you have set. The interest in insider research is percolating into colleges and universities from the action research movement within schools and may grow at a comparable rate.

Insider Research and the Model of Reflection

Insider research is a form of participant research. It is principally about understanding and improving practice within the researcher's institution. It can be focused on a problem and involve cycles of data collection, evaluation and reflection, as in action research.

Insider research need not be problem-centred. It is an appropriate approach for a matter of personal curiosity or interest that you decide to investigate in a systematic way. Many tutors who have used the approach have found that insider research is an empowering process. It often comes up with surprises and enables you to see problems in new ways. It is probably the most effective way of exploring the functioning of real life classrooms and investigating the effects of your interventions. It deals with the real problems and issues you face and, in doing so, may transform those problems and the way you construe teaching and learning. It has a moral base, in that it allows you to explore your actions and those of others in the light of the values that supposedly underpin them.

The series is built on the model of the reflective practitioner of education as described by Dewey (1916) and developed by Zeichner, Ashcroft and others (see, for instance, Ashcroft, 1987; Ashcroft and Griffiths, 1989; Deakin, 1982; Isaac and Ashcroft, 1986; Stenhouse, 1979; Zeichner, 1982; and Zeichner and Teitlebaum, 1982). The model takes the view that knowledge is not absolute or static and that lecturers in further and higher education should take an active role in constructing and reconstructing it. This suggests that educationists have some sort of moral responsibility for the truth, and indeed that it is part of their duty to act as whistle-blowers when the powerful define truth in ways convenient for their purposes. It sees reflective practice as much more than a passive 'thinking about'. It embraces active professional development, directed at particular qualities: open-mindedness, commitment and responsibility. The enquiry considers the question of 'What works?' but also moves on to pose questions of worthwhileness. This demands investigation into action, intervention and the perspectives of a number of the participants in the educational process: students, tutors, institutional managers, employers, the government, funders and community representatives. It also suggests that intentions, attitudes and values are explored, as well as behaviour and outcomes.

Each of the qualities of open-mindedness, commitment and responsibility has particular definitions and demands prerequisite skills and understandings. This series of books is partially directed at helping you to acquire research skills and skills of analysis. Open-mindedness requires that you seek out and analyse the perspectives of each of the stakeholders in education. For this reason, this book includes a variety of examples of ways to collect and organize data that you might use to find out about the behaviours, thoughts, attitudes and experience of students, other lecturers, managers, employers and others. In Chapter 3 we suggest that you might use group interviews to find out the definitions of 'good' assessment favoured by various of the stakeholders in education. Our intention in introducing you to various research processes is to enable you to collect data and to analyse them in the light of your emerging theory of practice (see Argyris and Schon, 1974, for more details of this notion of theory in action.)

Commitment implies a real and sustained attachment to the value of your work and to improving its context. You need optimism in order to sustain this: to believe that you are one of the stakeholders in the institution and community, and that you have the duty and power to effect changes and to secure the appropriate teaching and learning environment for your students. This is not easy, particularly in circumstances where resources are very short or where you work within an autocratic or chaotic management regime. Insider research cannot solve these kinds of problems, but it may help you to understand their nature and go some way to helping you to cope. For example, in Chapter 5 we suggest a method for exploring the lecturer's use of time. From this kind of investigation you may be able to see ways that limited time might be used more effectively and the stress caused by time pressures reduced.

Responsibility implies that you are interested in the long- and short-term consequences of action. This means that you collect evidence as to your effectiveness and the intended and unintended outcomes of your teaching and management. We suggest a range of research instruments that may help you to discover what you actually do (as opposed to what you think you do) in the course of your work, what effects your behaviour has on others, how they see it and the attitudes resulting from it. For instance, in Chapter 6, we suggest a model for exploring the effects of an educational innovation on student skills, knowledge and attitude development.

Insider research can be empowering. It is one way of finding out about the needs and interests of others and expressing these in terms that create a powerful case for change. For this reason, we have included a range of starting points for research that will enable you to enquire into management issues and the working of your institution.

We have stated that research skills are an essential prerequisite to reflective practice. This should not be taken to mean that they are sufficient. Reflective practice in teaching also requires that you acquire a range of other skills. These include technical teaching skills, such as voice projection; interpersonal skills such as counselling skills and the ability to work as part of a team; communication skills in a variety of contexts; and the ability to criticize the status quo from a moral point of view. Insider research, perhaps uniquely, can help you to acquire each of these skills. By providing feedback on your actions, insider research directs you to problems that you are creating or failing to solve. You can then experiment with new ways of approaching them and use insider research to provide information on the effectiveness of your new ways of thinking and acting. In Chapter 7 we suggest a range of evaluation methods that you may want to use in order to explore your practice and that of others.

Reflective practice is an ideal that can be at its most painful when it is achieved. It requires that you question your deepest beliefs and compare your actions with your values. In doing this, you may find that you must abandon cherished beliefs or practices. Despite the loss that change brings and the risks that it involves, the value of reflective practice is in the process of continual questioning and renewal that is essential for professional development and growth in understanding. Nobody is able to sustain reflective practice at all times. During the process of teaching and research you will sometimes delude yourself. You may frame your problem according to assumptions that you feel comfortable with, you may interpret data to fit your preferred solution, or you may fail to notice the most important data. For this reason, we suggest that your methods and interpretation should be made public in some way. You need other people to challenge your assumptions.

Research in Colleges and Universities

In the UK, the proportion of young people going into higher education has doubled in recent years. When the members of this educated population enter colleges and universities, they expect to be taught by people who are expert at a very high level. This expertise is generally achieved through research and publication or through higher degree work that involves research. Education at this level is being seen as an increasingly rigorous process. Quality and standards in the sector have come under continuous scrutiny. One of the determinants in the assessment of quality is the level of expertise of staff. Staff who aspire to promotion may have to obtain higher level qualifications that include substantial research (Ashcroft and Foreman-Peck, 1994).

The growth of the pool of highly educated people means that there is increasing competition for permanent posts in colleges and universities. These posts usually go to those who can provide evidence that they are more expert than their competitors. In the UK, the numbers of staff on fixed term contracts in universities and colleges is growing. In the USA, a glut of highly educated professors means that the proportion of part-time staff in colleges and universities has doubled in the last 20 years (Irwin, 1995). The emphasis in universities on research ratings and the decision in many Western countries to make these public has created a 'publish or die' culture. University lecturers are expected to publish papers and books with increasing regularity. Where colleges aspire to include higher level courses within their portfolio, they often find that the staff who teach such courses are expected to demonstrate a research record that equals that of colleagues in the university sector.

Busy lecturers need to find a time-efficient way to research and publish. If you engage in insider research, you are likely to find your results are interesting and that they might have more general application. A number of my colleagues who engage in fairly small-scale research of this type, mainly for their own interest, have then published the resulting papers in refereed journals. For instance, I became interested in the process of developing criteria for the assessment of student teacher competence in classrooms. Discussions with colleagues and the collection of a variety of data led to the conclusion that the establishment of clear criteria for the assessment of teaching was by no means a matter of creating a simple checklist of indicators of appropriate action. My colleague and I were able to publish a paper outlining our small-scale study and conclusions in a refereed, international journal (Ashcroft and Tann, 1988).

6

In effect, I am suggesting 'quick and dirty' research as appropriate for the hard-working lecturer who wants to improve his or her practice. This can be somewhat refined and elaborated for publication. There is interest from editors and readers of journals in small-scale, modest research that focuses on the real dilemmas that lecturers face. On the other hand, insider research does have its weaknesses. In particular it is prone to self-justification and can be very inward-looking. If you are to be a successful insider researcher, you will need to identify a *critical* group or community that will help you identify appropriate research questions, refine your research instruments and evaluate your reflections and data as you go along. You will also need to seek alternative interpretations of your data from a number of sources and to read widely, in order to locate your insights in a wider context.

When I have engaged in this kind of research and publication, the key thing I have discovered is the need to relate my findings to a theoretical framework (see, for instance, Ashcroft and Griffiths, 1990 or Ashcroft and Peacock, 1993). Very occasionally, I have developed my own framework, but more usually I have used an existing one to analyse my findings. Without such analysis, the results of insider research tend to be anecdotal and descriptive. Such work may be publishable, but in magazines and newspapers, rather than research journals.

Starting Points for Research: Values and Practice

We do not provide a total blueprint for research. A large part of the new knowledge and understanding gained from research comes from the stimulus to creativity that asking your own questions and looking at preliminary data provide. In collecting your own data and then asking questions of yourself, you will come up with transformational resolutions to research questions that are far more innovative and creative than any the authors could suggest. Therefore, you should feel free to interpret research tasks widely: to adapt and alter suggested foci for research and ideas for data collection to fit your own context and, most importantly, to go beyond the first cycle of data collection to ask your own questions.

It is important to be aware of the limitations of small-scale research. If you claim a spurious objectivity to your work, you are likely to miss the most important strength of small-scale research: the opportunity it offers to you to explore your existing practice and that of others, the stated values that underpin this practice and the relationship between those values and the practice. Practice may seem to you to be the most objective of these elements but, in exploring practice, it is important to realize that it is often more difficult to get at it than first appears. There is often a gap between what people (including you) say and believe that they do and what they actually do. Thus, self-report may not capture the data you need. Other methods are mediated by the values of the person undertaking the analysis.

Each of us has values that we espouse. Many teachers can articulate them in relation to certain criteria. For example, most of us believe in equal opportunity. You may want to dig deeper than this to explore how equal opportunities are defined by teachers and how these definitions are or may be incompatible. The series explores the values that are held by each of the stakeholders in education, the implications of these for teaching, learning and management, and the extent to which they are compatible or raise dilemmas that must be resolved.

Perspectives to be Researched

Reflective practice is about taking account of the viewpoints of others and the long- as well as the short-term consequences of your action. For this reason, the series covers the investigation of a variety of perspectives, including:

- students;
- lecturers;
- providers of educational support services;
- institutional managers;
- employers;
- funders; and
- the local community.

Each of these groups has its own priorities and the people working within them have their own satisfactions and frustrations. The quality of the services that an institution provides in support of student learning is in part determined by these perspectives. For example, in Chapter 5 we suggest that you look at the influence of tutor practice on the admission of non-traditional students.

Research Issues Covered in the Books

A range of research issues are suggested within each book in the series. One of the most important of these is intimately related to values and practice: the perceptions of each of the stakeholders in education of various aspects of the educative process. Perceptions are closely related to attitudes, in that attitudes are the filter through which we see and judge reality. Attitudes are central to motivation and so to learning. This book will enable you to start to explore the attitudes of each of the stakeholders towards aspects of evaluation and assessment.

The link between attitudes and behaviour may be more or less direct. Actual behaviour is influenced by beliefs, but does not always seem compatible with those beliefs. Reflective practice explores the gap and the link between beliefs, implicit theories of teaching and learning, and actual behaviour. In Chapter 5 we suggest that you might explore the link between the lecturer's beliefs about their role in fostering students development in the non-cognitive domain and the assessment methods that they use.

Attitudes, perceptions and behaviour are part of the cocktail that influences educational priorities. The educational and non-educational priorities of each of the stakeholders in education are interesting in themselves, and also in the extent to which they are compatible. Understanding competing priorities can sometimes transform a seeming dilemma and enable new ways forward to be found. Moral choice becomes more possible when these are understood. For example, in Chapter 5 we suggest an exploration of the opportunity costs of non-traditional forms of assessment that has at its heart values about the educative process held by various stakeholders in education.

Typically, at a time of limited resources, prioritization focuses upon the different value given to efficiency and effectiveness. Efficiency and effectiveness are highly topical concerns in colleges and universities. Each may be measured in different ways and each will affect all aspects of the students' learning experience. For example, we invite you to investigate the tensions between efficiency and effectiveness as they relate to assessment and to underlying political purposes and values.

Behind almost every controversy in education are differences in definitions of the problems education faces and the criteria by which success or failure in dealing with these problems may be judged. Because these definitions intimately affect any judgements made, objectivity in educational research must be a false goal. The strength of insider research is that it can recognize and explore ambiguity. The investigations within this book may help you to explore and articulate the values that underpin criteria and definitions used in judgement. For instance, we look at concepts of reliability and validity in assessment, and invite you to consider how the political climate influences how these are defined.

The educative process can be looked at in terms of its objectives, processes or outcomes. Each of these imply a different view of what education is about. Each is worth exploring in its own right and from the point of view of the various parties. The most interesting investigation may be into the compatibility of each with the others in real classroom conditions, For example, we suggest that you might explore evaluation models that are based on processes and outcomes. Which you value will depend on your ideas about the purposes of education.

Education is a complex interactive human process. For this reason it depends in a fundamental way on relationships between people. Each party to and group concerned with education is affected by the others. The complexity of this interaction and the effects that it has upon teaching and learning are therefore central concerns of the book. For example, in Chapter 3 we suggest that the lecturer should be concerned with, and might wish to investigate, the operation of institutional quality assurance systems and the values that underpin them.

If you believe that reflective practice requires the teacher to take a moral stance, some positions, such as that of a racist standpoint, are incompatible with reflective practice. Justice, equality and the ways that diversity is catered for within education therefore become important areas of investigation. This investigation of the morality of the educative process and institutional function can take many forms. In order to take issues of justice and fairness seriously, you have to consider conflicting interests within education. For example, you may need to consider how practical knowledge and skill can be accredited, if able students who missed out on educational opportunities when they were young are to be admitted to educational programmes that could benefit them.

Ethics and control issues in learning draw a number of issues together. The exploration of dilemmas, how they are construed by the various parties, the way that good practice might be defined, the way that interests compete and are resolved, raise ethical issues, often closely related to the exercise of power and control. Each of the books in the series explores issues of ethics and control across all of the subject matter that they explore. It is this concern, and the willingness to face the difficult problems that result from it, that characterizes reflective practice.

The Quantitative and Qualitative Research Tradition

Research in education may fall into the quantitative tradition and focus on the collection (usually of large numbers) of numerical data, or into the qualitative tradition and look in depth at a smaller number of instances. It may be focused on discovery or on the improvement of practice.

There is much ideological baggage that now surrounds the qualitative and quantitative traditions in education. You need to get to grips with this debate in order to understand the strengths and weaknesses of each. Within education there has been a shift from respect for models of research based on the scientific tradition of experimental and quasi-experimental research methods, towards qualitative, descriptive methods within naturalistic settings, first pioneered in subjects such as anthropology and now termed ethnographic methods. Each of these models has its strengths and weaknesses. The qualitative tradition is criticized because of its limited scope, particularity and subjectivity; the quantitative tradition because of the triviality of its findings, their lack of application to the real life messiness of classrooms and because most practitioners of such research were expert in research, not in education, and therefore spoke to other researchers rather than to teachers.

Quantitative research must be judged in its own terms. For instance, questions of usefulness or applicability may not be to the point. Quantitative research is 'good' research if the results are valid and reliable. Reliability (the extent to which the context and results can be replicated) is sometimes overemphasized at the expense of other aspects of validity, such as the assumptions underpinning the questions asked and categories used.

Research in the qualitative tradition must also be judged by appropriate criteria. It should not be criticized for subjectivity, unless it claims to be objective. Such research is often problem-centred and pragmatic, and so the notion of proof becomes irrelevant. The validity of the research depends on the extent that the situation, actions, causes and effects are described convincingly. The quality of the research may depend on interjudgemental reliability (do the readers, researchers and the actors in the research situation describe and interpret the findings in the same way?) Subjective factors are taken into account in judging its quality: at a pragmatic level (was the problem solved to the satisfaction of all the parties involved?); and at a moral level (the moral basis of actions by the researcher is often open to scrutiny – did they ask the right question, were they up front about their thoughts, feelings and motives, were the values that underpinned the research made explicit?)

Quantitative research methods in education make claims to reliability because of some kind of objectivity or because the test used has been found to work similarly in other situations (for instance, by other researchers, against other tests, and so on). External validity (the extent to which the results of a study can be generalized to other times and places) is generally a matter of the situation and population studied: the size of sample, its typicality and the categories used. Campbell and Stanley (1963) give one of the best outlines of factors that commonly jeopardize the validity of such research. The researcher may present him or herself as a detached outsider observing a situation or seeking to disprove a hypothesis. Thus, some attempt may be made to control the variables in the situation and many instances of a particular result may be described before it can be considered significant. Statistical significance is determined by a standard statistical test.

The kind of insider research that may be most appropriate to reflective practice occasionally uses experimental methods and 'soft' quantitative techniques, but relies more heavily on the qualitative research tradition. It makes few claims for reliability and external validity. Instead, it seeks to describe a particular situation in all its complexity. For this reason, the control of variables is usually inappropriate. The reader determines whether the results are, or are not, relevant. In order that the reader can answer the question, Might this research have some significance to me in my particular situation?, they must know the author's claims to expert knowledge, the extent to which his or her conclusions and interpretation of the situation have been tested against the interpretations of other parties, the assumptions that the researcher made, and his or her emotional responses to issues and those of others. Elliott (1991) provides a good account of the strengths and weaknesses of research within the qualitative research tradition.

Each of the traditions makes its own assumptions about cause and effect. One model tidies and simplifies reality in order to look at and analyse it. In the other, the full messiness of reality is explored. The quantitative tradition tends to be inductive and the qualitative tradition deductive. What is important is that, whatever methods you use, you take the time to find out about the construction of appropriate research instruments and admit to the threats to the validity and reliability of the findings inherent within the approach you take.

Data Collection Techniques

The authors provide you with starting points only for research. There is a very wide range of research methods open to you, including:

- questionnaires (structured, semi-structured and open-ended);
- standardized tests;

- interviews (structured, semi-structured and open-ended, individual and group);
- observation techniques (structured, semi-structured and open-ended);
- scenario analysis;
- biographical analysis;
- diaries and field notes;
- systems analysis;
- document analysis; and
- video, audio and photographic analysis.

The advantages and problems of each of these methods are described in the introductory chapter of Bennett *et al.* (1996). They may be used separately, or in conjunction, to create the fuller picture that is required of a case study.

Most of the research suggested in the series is small-scale and local and so we do not discuss methods of statistical analysis. It may be that you become inspired to undertake a more major study, in which case there are a variety of computer programs that may help you to analyse your data (see for instance, Bennett *et al.*, 1996 for more detail on the use of information technology for qualitative data analysis), or you may find a book such as Cohen and Manion (1985) useful. If you intend to use statistical analysis, it is important that you make this decision at the start of the data collection process. The method you use will affect the form of the data you should collect. You will probably find all sorts of problems if you collect your data and then look round for a means of analysing it.

The important thing is never to claim more for your research than is justified by your methods, the data you have collected and your analysis. For instance, it would not be wise to claim a breakthrough if you took up the suggestion in Chapter 6 and participated in a peer review of teaching and found that your impressions of lessons were in accord with those of colleagues. Small-scale research is unlikely to push back the frontiers of knowledge, but it can sometimes empower the reader, who may be inspired by a report of research into practice that chimes with their own experience. It is almost impossible to prove anything in education. You need to be very tentative in your conclusions. Because it is almost impossible to isolate variables in real educational situations, it is seldom possible to say that a particular stimulus *caused* a particular *effect*. Even if you get apparently clear-cut results, generally the best that can be said is that, in the circumstances you investigated, it appears that one thing may be *associated* with another.

Annotated Reading List

Andresen, L *et al.* (1993) *Strategies for Assessing Students*, Birmingham: Staff
and Educational Development Association.
A guide to managing assessment as part of teaching.

Angelo, TA and Cross, K P (1993) *Classroom Assessment Techniques: A handbook
for college teachers*, London: Jossey-Bass.
A good source of pro formas and ideas for looking at assessment.

Argyris, C and Schon, D (1974) *Theory into Practice*, Beckenham: Croom Helm.
The definitive book on the relationships between the theories that people
hold about their teaching and the theories that they develop in action.

Ashworth, A and Harvey, R (1993) *Quality in Further and Higher Education*,
London: Jessica Kingsley.
An account of Total Quality Management, performance indicators, and
systems for assessing standards.

Brown, S and Dove, P (eds) (1990) *Self and Peer Assessment*, Birmingham: Staff
and Educational Development Association.
This is a useful book that covers most peer and self-assessment methods.
The focus is on 'how to do it' rather than 'how to research it', but you
may find some of the types of assessment described useful as the basis of
categories in your research.

Brown, S, Jones, G and Rawnsley, S (eds) (1993) *Observing Teaching*,
Birmingham: Staff and Educational Development Association.
This focuses on inquiring into practice in colleges and universities. It
covers issues in the appraisal of teaching: who should do it, what should
be observed and how. The focus is on professional development, rather
than research within higher education.

Bell, J (1987) *Doing your Research Project*, Buckingham: Open University Press.
This book deals with research across the disciplines, rather than teaching
and learning in further and higher education.

Cohen, L and Manion, L (1985) *Research Methods in Education*, 2nd edn,
Beckenham: Croom Helm.
A comprehensive account of the major research methods in education. It
is not easy to read, and I would argue with its assumption that educational
research should be scientific, but its critique of the approach we adopt
provides a useful counterbalance. The book covers most of the techniques
in educational research, as well as more technical aspects such as grid
analysis and multidimensional measurement.

Gibbs, G (ed) (1984 and 1985) *Alternatives in Assessment 1* and *Alternatives in
Assessment 2*, Birmingham: Staff and Educational Development Association.
Case studies of different methods of assessment found in higher
education only.

Gibbs, G *et al. 53 Interesting Things to do...*, Bristol: TES.
This series is very popular and sells well. The focus is on practice, rather
than research, but this can provide you with a starting point for an
evaluation or intervention study.

Green, D (1993) *What is Quality in Higher Education?*, Buckingham: Open University Press.
A report of a national research project on the assessment of quality in higher education only.
Hammersley, M and Atkinson, P (1983) *Ethnography Principles in Practice*, London: Tavistock.
A reasonably accessible account of ethnographic methods and their relationship to the social world. It includes a critical analysis of case study, observation, interviewing and ways of filing and recording data.
McKernan, J (1991) *Curriculum Action Research: A Handbook of Methods and Resources for the Reflective Practitioner*, London: Kogan Page.
This book is a good introduction to action research. It contains many useful suggestions for collecting data.
Smith, B and Brown, S (eds) (1994) *Research, Teaching and Learning in Higher Education*, London: Kogan Page.
A collection of reports of research undertaken by experienced education developers within higher education.
Thorpe, M (1993) *Evaluating Open and Distance Learning*, Harlow: Longman
Covers how to evaluate one type of learning programme.

References

Argyris, C and Schon, D (1974) *Theory into Practice*, Beckenham: Croom Helm.
Ashcroft, K (1987) 'The history of an innovation', *Assessment and Evaluation in Higher Education*, 12, 1, 37–45.
Ashcroft, K and Foreman-Peck, L (1994) *Managing Teaching and Learning in Further and Higher Education*, London: Falmer Press.
Ashcroft, K and Foreman-Peck, L (1995) *The Lecturer's Guide to Quality and Standards in Colleges and Universities*, London: Falmer Press.
Ashcroft, K and Griffiths, M (1989) 'Reflective teachers and reflective tutors: School experience in an initial teacher education course', *Journal of Education for Teaching*, 15, 1, 35–52.
Ashcroft, K and Griffiths, M (1990) 'Action research in initial teacher education', in Zuber-Skerritt, O (ed.) *Action Research in Higher Education*, Brisbane: Griffith University Press.
Ashcroft, K and Peacock, E (1993) 'An evaluation of the progress, experience and employability of mature students on the BEd course at Westminster College, Oxford', *Assessment and Evaluation in Higher Education*, 18, 1, 57–70.
Ashcroft, K and Tann, S (1988) 'Beyond building a better checklist: development in a school experience programme', *International Journal of Assessment and Evaluation in Higher Education*, 13, 1, 61–72.
Ashcroft, K, Bigger, S and Coates, D (1996) *Researching into Equal Opportunities in Colleges and Universities*, London: Kogan Page.
Ashcroft, K, Jones, M and Siraj-Blatchford, J (1996) *Researching into Student Learning and Support in Colleges and Universities*, London: Kogan Page.

Bennett, C, Foreman-Peck, L and Higgins, C (1996) *Researching into Teaching Methods in Colleges and Universities,* London: Kogan Page.

Burgess, R (1984) 'Keeping a research diary', in Bell, J and Goulding, S (eds) *Conducting Small-scale Investigations in Education Management,* London: Harper and Row.

Campbell, DT and Stanley, JC (1963) *Experimental and Quasi-experimental Designs for Research,* Chicago, IL: Rand McNally.

Cohen, L and Manion, L (1985) *Research Methods in Education,* 2nd edn, Beckenham: Croom Helm.

Deakin University (1982) *The Action Research Reader,* Victoria: Deakin University Press.

Elliott, J (1991) *Action Research for Educational Change,* Buckingham: Open University Press.

Dewey, J. (1916) *Democracy and Education,* New York: The Free Press.

Irwin, A (1995) 'Gypsy professors roam US campuses', *The Times Higher Education Supplement,* 24 February.

Isaac, J and Ashcroft, K (1986) 'A leap into the practical', in Nias, J and Groundwater-Smith, S (eds) *The Enquiring Teacher: Supporting and sustaining teacher research,* London: Falmer Press.

Stenhouse, L (1979) 'What is action research?', CARE, University of East Anglia, mimeograph.

Zeichner, K and Teitlebaum, K (1982) 'Personalised and inquiry oriented education: an analysis of two approaches to the development of curriculum in field-based experience', *Journal of Education for Teaching,* 8, 2, 95–117.

Zeichner, K (1982) 'Reflective teaching and field-based experience in teacher education', *Interchange,* 12, 4, 1–22.

Chapter 2

The Purposes of Assessment

In this chapter we will discuss a number of issues relating to assessment, but the question which is fundamental to the notion of 'purpose', and therefore is addressed throughout the chapter, is: *Why do you assess your students?*

About 15 or so years ago, if you were to have asked many lecturers in UK further and, more particularly, higher education institutions why they assess students, their initial response may well have been a blank stare. For many lecturers the main purpose of assessment was quite clear and, relatively speaking, unproblematic: it was to collect marks, usually expressed in the form of percentages, so as to inform registrars (and ultimately students) of how well students had done in end of year or end of course examinations and, if relevant, which students could proceed to the next year of the course. Some lecturers were keen to know how well their students had done, but not all were particularly interested; it has to be remembered that the vast majority of lecturers had been recruited into higher education because of their interest in, and experience of, undertaking academic, usually subject-based, research. Somehow, for students to do well in examinations was a reflection on the teaching abilities of lecturers; on the other hand if students did badly, it was a reflection on their own inattentiveness and lack of hard work, especially revision.

In the UK at that time many courses, particularly those in institutions now called 'the old universities', tended to be academic in orientation with little attention being given to meeting the needs of either students or commerce and industry. Education, apart from certain areas such as medicine and to some extent engineering, was perceived to be a 'good thing'; it was for the inner person and was seen by many lecturers as being of little direct relevance to students' future needs including those which were related to adult life and the world of work. It was a system which, in the main, viewed students as passive learners, and the government, through the public purse, as the unquestioning supplier of the resources necessary to enable universities and colleges to organize the

17

courses which they thought fit to provide. Despite its many and various pleas to make higher education more relevant to the world of work, the government of the day appeared resigned to leaving education in the hands of the professionals.

The view that post-compulsory education was remote from the needs of young adults (and most students were under 25) and the world of work, and that it appeared not to want to listen to the pleas from successive governments and from industrialists is, perhaps, a generalized and cynical analysis of the situation in the UK around 1980. Nevertheless, it was a view which at the time the government was putting across with increasing conviction and, what is more, it was a view which was being listened to by the electorate with increasing sympathy. This situation was not confined, of course, to the post-compulsory education system in the UK; it merely mirrored what was happening in many other countries of the developed world. Furthermore, the general approach adopted by institutions of higher education merely reflected, according to the government and industry, a continuation of what was happening in secondary schools in the UK.

The Context for Assessment

The need to improve Britain's standing in the commercial and industrial world was not a belief born out of the 1980s; nor was the view that this poor standing was due to the lack of a well-motivated, highly trained and skilled workforce, which was, in turn, the fault of the educational systems to be found in the UK. What was new to the mid-1980s scene was the strategy through which the government intended to remedy this situation. The way in which the government saw further and higher education delivering a workforce equipped with the knowledge, skills and attitudes necessary for the modern, competitive and highly technological market place necessitated the government abandoning its traditional hands-off approach to post-compulsory education.

The situation in the UK came to a head with the publication of the Great Education Reform Bill – Gerbil for short – and, in 1988, with the passing of the Education Reform Act. For schools and higher education institutions and, through subsequent Education Acts, colleges of further education, a major underlying principle of these government-led initiatives was *accountability for funds made available by the Treasury*: in other words, public accountability for public money.

Assessments of what students know, understand and can do, being, perhaps, the main measurable outcomes of the education process which could be made available to the public most easily, were no longer to be considered a private affair between lecturers and their students: now these outcomes had to be made available to anyone with an interest in knowing what education had 'produced'. (The term 'stakeholder', as used in the context of stocks and shares, came to be used to describe any person or organization with an interest in, or a justifiable claim to need to know, the outcomes of the educational process.) Education Acts from 1988 onward had the effect of making institutions from nursery schools to postgraduate research centres more accountable for how they spent public funds. In theory, at least, this could mean any taxpayer had a right to know that her or his money has been spent wisely; in practice this position has been taken to mean the elected government, and any organization with a much more direct interest than the general public in what the outcomes of education are. However, the public was to be kept informed, in the case of schools and colleges of further education, through the publication of league tables of performance and, in the case of higher education, through the publication of separate quality ratings for teaching and research.

Two new tenets became uppermost in the government's mind: value for money – whether or not the 'agreed' outcomes were produced at the right price, and fitness for intended purpose – whether or not these outcomes were what they really ought to be. Underlying the first tenet are issues of quality and standards; underlying the second is the issue of relevance. Increasingly, the government was stating, and the electorate was listening to and agreeing with, opinions which had as an underlying principle: 'Don't listen to the professionals, they are trying to protect their privileged position; trust us since it is only we who know what is best for Britain'.

In essence, government initiatives over the past eight to ten years have led to the emergence of a new term – stakeholder – and a redefinition of an already existing concept – purpose. (The meaning of 'purpose' was modified to take account of the fact that the outcomes of assessment were now to be made public.) Because accountability for the outcomes of the educational system was now to the public in general, more people wanted a direct say, and had a legal right to have their views taken into account, when the purposes of the educational system at every level were being discussed and determined. In the government's mind, meeting the needs of the labour market so as to maintain the UK's competitiveness in world trading, became a major, if not the major, purpose of education from the age of 14 upwards.

Assessment and Purpose

Within the space of a few years the number of people entering higher education in the UK, as elsewhere in the world, more or less doubled and at the moment about one in three 18-year-olds is in higher education – a remarkable achievement in its own right yet still some way behind most other countries in the developed world, notably Germany, the USA and Japan. However, this increase in student numbers was not matched by a comparable increase in funding from the UK government – the expansion in numbers coincided with a deep and lasting recession in the world economy. At first institutions expanded so as to meet consumer (student) demand – meeting consumer demand was a fundamental tenet of the government's economic and social policies. Unfortunately, the demand from students was for courses leading to arts and humanities degrees; the demand was not for science, engineering and technology courses as intended originally by the government if the perceived industrial and economic skills shortages were to be met. The government felt it needed to be in the driving seat and this in turn required it to adopt a more hands-on approach to post-compulsory education, a point that has been made already in the introduction to this chapter. Ideas such as meeting consumer demand, identification of quality and its reward, value added and value for money, were all spawned out of a desire to ensure that education 'delivered the goods': namely that the UK entered the twenty-first century from a position of commercial and industrial strength.

Many people in education, and as time went by, an increasing number of people outside of further and higher education, disagreed with the view that an educational system based on these ideas would deliver the government's intention to achieve a well-motivated, skilled workforce. Furthermore, even if the ideas were accepted as the way forward, there was no shared understanding of their precise meaning. For example, a very good and detailed discussion of the meaning of quality as applied to the further and higher education system, and in particular the relationships which exist now between assessment and quality, can be found in a paper by Harvey and Green (1993). They list six different meanings of quality, each one of which might constitute a basis for measures of how well institutions were meeting the government's demands to demonstrate quality. However, we will not pursue this point here, since researching the relationship between assessment and quality is the subject of the next chapter in this book.

Today, in many countries of the developed world, post-compulsory education is an opportunity to which many people aspire; it is no longer an entitlement for a select few – the so-called academic elite. The expansion in student numbers referred to earlier, coupled with a more 'hands-on' approach by the government, has seen some significant changes to the purposes and direction of the post-compulsory education system in the UK. While a few courses have remained unchanged, many courses, in both further education and higher education, have been modified, in terms of content and approaches to teaching and assessment, so as to be more closely in tune with these government-led initiatives. Many institutions responded to the opportunities offered by the new directions and the increase in student numbers by developing completely new courses, often in modular format; for example, business studies, humanities and media studies.

At the beginning of this chapter we asked why lecturers assess their students. Now that we have explored some of the current major issues affecting education in industrialized societies, admittedly from a UK perspective, you might like to consider the question again and to explore the issues in more detail.

RESEARCH TASK. WHY DO YOU ASSESS YOUR STUDENTS?

Find out:

- Who makes use of the assessment information which you collect about your students?
- To which organizations is information sent concerning the assessment outcomes of your students?
- For what purposes, and in what formats, do these organizations need this information?

Find out what information agencies both inside and outside your institution require and what use they make of it. Find out if there is any difference between the type of information that is required on a routine basis and information that is required for a specific purpose, for example, visits by central government or other funding agency inspectors or assessors.

To obtain a comprehensive list of organizations you may need to meet with a number of managers in your institution and to ask them the questions mentioned above. Managers you might find it helpful to consult with include:

- course leaders;
- heads of department/faculty;
- finance;
- quality assurance;
- marketing;
- registry.

This questioning should give you a good working knowledge of *what is*. It is unlikely to provide you with in-depth information concerning the reasons and/or contexts for the collection of this assessment information nor is it likely to provide you with information concerning either *what was* or *what will/might be*. For information of this nature you may need to undertake an analysis of documents which outline what is required of institutions. The documents which you are likely to find most useful are those produced by organizations such as central government funding agencies. Discussing this matter with managers from within your institution should give you a very good indication of which documents it would be useful to consult.

Evidence and Purpose

An analysis of the reasons why students are assessed and the uses to which assessment information are put is likely to reveal that different purposes require different sorts of evidence to be collected. Therefore, the purposes underpinning the collection of assessment information are almost certainly going to determine not only what types of student assignments are set but also the different assessment processes and procedures that are necessary to collect the full range of information that is required. The dilemmas which this might throw up for an assessment programme were first identified in a report on the assessment arrangements in respect of the National Curriculum in English and Welsh schools, published by the DES and WO in 1988. One of the questions identified in this report, and which centred on the issue of purpose, was, how can a single assessment be used for both comparative (summative) and diagnostic (formative) purposes? This question poses a fundamental and intractable issue which needs to be addressed before any assessment system which purports to achieve both objectives is put into place. However, the government chose to play down the importance of this question since it put obstacles in the way of the proposals for a national assessment system in schools which was intended to be both comparative (for use in the compilation of leagues tables of schools, for example) *and* diagnostic (to aid student learning). An excellent critique of the National Curriculum assessment system in England and Wales, especially in respect of issues relating to the validity and reliability of assessments, can be found in Murphy (1988). Reading this article should provide you with useful background information for when you come to consider matters relating to the assessment programme for the courses you teach.

In the next research task you will be to asked select one of the courses you teach on and to identify the various stakeholders and the differing types of information that they might require. Without preempting the outcomes of this research, you are likely to find that two important stakeholders are the students themselves and the funders of the course. Students in general are most likely to want their assessment programme to provide, at significant points in their course, information of two distinct types. First, a description of what they have achieved, and by implication what they still need to achieve, often expressed in terms of either specific criteria or statements of competence – what is known as criterion-referenced assessment. Second, a description of what they have achieved at the end of their course usually, though not necessarily, expressed in a form that relates their achievements to those of other students on the same, or a comparable, course. In other words, students are likely to be looking for detailed, qualitative statements concerning their achievements at regular intervals throughout the course (what is known as formative or diagnostic assessment), together with statements at the end of the course which summarize their overall achievements (summative assessment).

The agencies which fund courses, and especially those of central government, are often interested in quality (however defined), value for money and issues to do with standards in education – usually their maintenance but even better their enhancement. To meet these requirements funding agencies are likely to require data which enable them to compare one institution with another at any given point in time, and to compare the performance of each institution over a period of time. For purposes such as these, simple, summary data presented in quantifiable form, such as the percentage of students being awarded a first class honours degree are required. Therefore, to meet the needs of central government, in particular, institutions are required to collect data of a different sort to that required by students. For central government, institutions need to collect global assessment data, such as marks out of one hundred, which have compared one student with another so that all students, once the marks for the whole course have been collated, may be assigned to predetermined categories: this is known as norm-referenced assessment.

In other words, because of the interest which central governments have in accountability, institutions in many countries are being encouraged to report simple, readily available quantitative measures (which have the merit of being high on reliability but unfortunately low on validity) at the expense of complex individualized qualitative assessments of the performance of that institution – the type of information which perhaps students and employers would prefer – based on professional judgement (which have the merit of being high on validity but unfortunately tend to suffer by being low on reliability) (Morrison *et al.*, 1995). The concerns over measures such as performance indicators and value added are not so much to do with whether or not these are appropriate measures for education but more to do with whether there is any consensus as to how they may be defined, whether they can be measured in a reliable and valid way, and whether the effects – any changes in the performance of institution(s) – can be assigned unambiguously to a cause (Hadley and Winn, 1992).

RESEARCH TASK. WHO ARE THE STAKEHOLDERS IN ASSESSMENT?

Choose one of the courses which you teach on. List all the people or groups of people you think are the stakeholders of that course; ask yourself why they might have an interest in the course.

Ask as many of your stakeholders as possible the following two questions. Try to ensure that you talk with at least one representative from each category of stakeholder. (You may need to explain to them the meaning of the term stakeholder.)

- Who do you consider to be a stakeholder of this course?
- Why do you consider these people to be stakeholders, ie, what criteria are you applying?

Ask anyone who does not include themself why they have done this.

Use your results as the basis for an enquiry into the definitions of 'valid stakeholder' put forward by various organizations involved in further and higher education.

The Perspectives of Stakeholders

Not everyone in education, and here you may need to include yourself, is comfortable with the term stakeholder (you might like to investigate whether people find 'client' more acceptable), nor with the expanded group of people to whom this term now refers. Some people may not be aware that today the meaning of the word has changed so as to include a wider set of people than it did a few years ago. So, it might be profitable to ask colleagues in your institution the two questions in the research task above. Is it appropriate to consider people from within your own institution, for example, a course leader, a head of department/dean of faculty, a college principal/university vice-chancellor, as being a stakeholder? If the answer is 'Yes', then in what capacity, and under what conditions, are they defined as a stakeholder? If the answer is 'No', then is it possible to consider them as being a manager acting on behalf of a stakeholder, for example one of the central government funding agencies, or another provider of funds to run the course?

Having identified who the various stakeholders are, you will be in a position to ask questions of each stakeholder – or at least as many of them as you can talk with in person – concerning the types of information that they would like to know about a course and/or the students on that course, and whether or not they feel that they are receiving this information at the moment.

RESEARCH TASK. EXPLORING THE PERSPECTIVES OF STAKEHOLDERS IN ASSESSMENT

Based on the information gained in the previous research task, make a list of all the stakeholders of a course you teach on.

Now ask representatives from each category of stakeholder what sorts of assessment or evaluation information they would like to receive from your institution. Before you do this you may find it helpful to return to the first research task in this chapter and to ask each stakeholder what they consider the purposes of the assessment programme to be.

You may find it difficult to obtain directly the sorts of information you are seeking from course funders, especially those associated with central government. You may need to talk to the people in your institution who have responsibility for sending the various numerical and other returns to course funders, for example, central government funding agencies, employers and, in the UK, local education authorities.

Use the information you have collected as the basis for a discursive paper which describes:

● the work that you have done;
● the ways in which the course assessment programme meets the needs of the various stakeholders with whom you have consulted;
● the potential, or actual, tensions that may arise because of the differing demands from individual stakeholders which have to be addressed through the assessment programme;
● the plan of action, assuming that one is possible, that you propose to put forward to address these tensions.

Assuming your proposal for change is approved by course managers, put your proposal into effect and, at the same time, undertake a further piece of research which evaluates the effectiveness of the measures you have implemented; see Chapter 7 for more information on how you might do this.

Data gathered as a result of undertaking the research task above may well reveal the need for additional assessment information about students which, although not provided at the moment, could be supplied were the assessment programme to be suitably modified. If you identify this type of situation, you may find it helpful to consider some of the questions raised in Chapter 4, particularly those in the section dealing with mapping assessment criteria to course aims and objectives; completing the current task should help you address this new situation. Equally, you may find that some information, available fairly readily at the moment, is not being communicated to those stakeholder(s) who have expressed an interest in it. If you find yourself in this situation it may not be a matter of changing your assessment programme but of changing your reporting procedures so as to meet the needs of stakeholders. You might like to investigate how your reporting procedures could be modified so as to ensure that the needs of stakeholders are met.

Assessment and Student Learning

In this section we will look at two different views of assessment and how they impinge upon student learning; both views have a direct bearing on the question of the purpose of assessment. The first view of assessment requires students to demonstrate what they know, understand and can do already; assessment is seen as being quite separate from learning. In the second view, assessment is seen as being, in itself, a learning experience; in other words, assessment and learning are integral and inseparable parts of the same enterprise.

The first view of assessment comes to the fore at clearly defined and significant points in a course, for example at the end of a module, end of a year, and end of a course. Such a view is embodied in many timed, written examinations but it can also be seen in those formative assignments which, in the main, require students simply to give back to the lecturer what he or she has previously given to them. Assignments which mainly test students' recall of the content of a series of lectures and seminars are prime examples of this view. Assessment is seen as measuring a product only and as such it aims to find out what each student individually has achieved already: assessment is concerned with the creation of a summative description of learning. This is the traditional and, to many people, the more formal view of assessment; however, such a view may be extended so as to encompass some of the so-called modern approaches to assessment, such as the measurement of competences.

In the second view, assessment is not seen as simply measuring a product but is concerned also with the process of learning. In this approach to assessment students might be given a task to undertake which, in order to complete it successfully, will require them to acquire new learning – skills, attitudes, knowledge and understanding. However, any assessment of learning may still be only in terms of what has been produced and may not measure, in any direct way, any learning which has occurred during the completion of the task. In other words, the assessment measures the quality of the outcomes (products) of the task and not the processes which occurred along the way. Any assessment of the quality of the process necessary to complete the task, which is likely to be very difficult to achieve with any degree of objectivity, let alone on a percentage scale, may be either observed first-hand by the lecturer or inferred from the quality of the outcomes. Alternatively, 'process' may be assessed through self-completion student learning logs.

This second view is considered by many people to be a more progressive approach to assessment. It has commanded great popularity because incorporating it into an assessment programme can bestow a number of significant benefits, financial as well as educational: you might like to explore what these benefits are for students, lecturers and institutions. Equally, you might like to consider the costs of adopting such an approach; for instance, assessment resulting from the collection of first-hand evidence, like direct observation of the learning processes that occur during the completion of a task, is often a very time-consuming and unreliable way to proceed. For more details of the issues discussed so far in this section, and in particular how they relate to further and higher education, see Chapter 4.

RESEARCH TASK. ANALYSING ASSESSMENT TASKS IN TERMS OF OBJECTIVES

Select two assignments from a course on which you teach. One assignment should be selected because it reflects the first view of assessment mentioned above; this assignment could be an end of year examination. The other assignment should reflect the second view of assessment; this assignment might be a practical task undertaken collaboratively by a group of students. Consider each assignment in turn and ask yourself the following questions:

- What do you think each assignment is actually testing?
- What do you think are the strengths and weaknesses of each assignment?

Compare your answer to the first question with the course aims and objectives, and with any assessment criteria specified on the assignment sheet. In thinking about your answer to the second question, you might like to consider how, without significantly reducing the advantages, each assignment might be modified so as to address any perceived weaknesses. You may need to recognize that learning goes far beyond these stated learning objectives.

- Which learning objectives are specified implicitly within the assignment?
- Which learning objectives are unintended but nevertheless beneficial?

The section in Chapter 4 which discusses the mapping of assessment criteria to course aims and objectives should offer you some help in answering the questions raised so far.

Choose five or six students who have recently completed both assignments; ask each of them, either individually or in small groups, the same two questions you earlier asked yourself.

- What do students believe the two assignments are testing?
- What do students perceive to be the strengths and weaknesses of each assignment?

Now consider:

- the match between your perceptions of the strengths and weaknesses of both assignments and those of your students;
- any changes that you might wish to make so as to bring these perceptions closer together.

Introduce changes to the assignments in the light of the above analysis. (Before you do this you might like to consider the next research task.)

Monitor the changes you have introduced the next time students complete both assignments.

Write a paper which summarizes what you have found out and the effectiveness of the steps you have taken to address the issues uncovered.

Assessment and Motivation

Both of the views concerning the relationships between assessment and student learning outlined so far are what might be termed 'high minded'. At the heart of both views is the belief that students want to learn the things that lecturers want them to learn and that assessment is simply the means by which you, and your institution, demonstrate in an objective and impartial way that this learning has taken place. The motivation which enables students to learn is intrinsic – it comes from within them. Students, therefore, want to learn either because they find the course interesting in its own right or because they find what they are experiencing is of value or of use to them. Some people, perhaps some of your colleagues – even some of your students – may believe that such a view is a fairly enlightened one. Some of these people may feel that students learn only those aspects of the course which comprise the formal elements of the assessment programme. Put the other way around, if a part of a course were not assessed then students would not learn it; they may not even attend the sessions.

In this view, assessment is likely to be seen as a carrot (or is it a stick?) which enables students to progress through the course. The assessment programme provides much of the (extrinsic) motivation to learn. Courses where the predominant underlying belief is that assessment provides students with extrinsic motivation are likely to have an assessment programme which lays emphasis on formal written assignments and upon frequent use of unseen written tests and examinations, especially those where the range of questions encompasses only a fairly restricted range of the total syllabus covered. On the other hand, courses where students are expected to demonstrate that their motivation is intrinsic may tend to lay emphasis on learning through assessment and on group practical work – an example of what is sometimes called 'learning by doing'.

Your experience may suggest that students on the whole prefer their assignments to be intrinsically motivating. On the other hand, you may feel that within the assessment programme a balance needs to be struck between assignments which students find intrinsically motivating and those which motivate them through extrinsic means. This implies a variety of assessment (an idea that is developed further in Chapter 4) and of striking the appropriate balance. The difficulty in trying to shift the balance in an assessment programme towards a greater emphasis on intrinsic means of motivating students is that the situation can sometimes be self-reinforcing. Students on courses with a large number of written assignments may adopt, or may be encouraged to adopt, a fairly instrumental stance towards their progress and in the end only put effort into learning those aspects of their course which are required by the formal parts of the assessment programme.

In the UK, as elsewhere in the world, the expansion in the number of people entering post-compulsory education, higher education in particular, has, in many respects, been highly successful; a greater number of more highly and more relevantly skilled people are now entering the labour market. However, this increase has not been matched by a corresponding expansion in the numbers of appropriate job opportunities available. One consequence of this is 'overskilling' – that is, jobs which in the past would have been undertaken by people with (say) an advanced school leavers' certificate are now being undertaken by graduates; graduates are studying for postgraduate qualifications in order to obtain jobs which traditionally have been taken by graduates. Today, graduates who are unwilling, or unable, to undertake postgraduate level study or who are unwilling to step down in terms of career aspirations may find themselves unemployed; being successful on a course no longer guarantees securing a job appropriate to the level of experience or training. For many aspects of non-vocationally oriented post-compulsory education, higher education especially, motivation which derives its existence from outside the person has to give way to more internal forms of motivation. Students need to find personal satisfaction in a course of study, since at the end of their course there is no guarantee of a job. One way for students to achieve the desired level of personal satisfaction is through the assessment programme and the type of assignments you set them; this point is explored further in the following research task and in more detail in Chapter 4.

In the first task in this chapter, where the purposes of assessment were being explored, you may have identified 'providing students with the motivation to learn' as being one such purpose. However, if student motivation did not arise during the first research task then now might be an opportune moment to explore this issue. One reason for investigating assessment and its effects on student motivation is that to develop further your department's assessment practice, perhaps towards a greater use of non-written, collaborative styles of assessment, you may need to convince your colleagues that students will still learn – and learn well – even if they are not assessed in the same ways, or as frequently, as at present.

RESEARCH TASK. ANALYSING ASSESSMENT TASKS IN TERMS
OF MOTIVATION

Choose an assignment which you feel could be made more motivating for
students and a group of about six students who have completed this
assignment relatively recently. Students could be self-selected, but you need
to ensure that the group includes students who have put a lot of effort into
this assignment and others who have not. In other words, the group needs
to comprise both students who appear to be motivated as well as students
who, quite evidently, are not.

Ask students which aspects of the assignment they liked and which aspects
they did not. Now ask them to redesign the assignment to make it more
motivating for the next group of students. Before you set students off on this
task you will need to provide them with relevant details, such as what the
assignment is attempting to assess and the boundaries within which they may
work, including those aspects of the assignment which they may not change.
The overlap between this research task and the previous one is quite high;
perhaps they could be combined into one larger task?

The outcomes from this task could then form the basis for a departmental
paper in which you might first of all outline what you have done and what
you have found out, and then go on to develop a rationale for a revised
assessment programme for the relevant part(s) of the course under scrutiny.
What professional and/or institutional issues emerge from inviting students
to assist in the design of their assignments? You might like to include a
discussion of these in your paper.

An approach such as the one outlined in the research task above can be
a useful and productive way forward, especially if, as a more junior
member of department, you are trying to move things forward against
opposition from more senior colleagues. In situations like this you are
much more likely to get things moving in the direction desired if you
have some empirical evidence upon which to base a proposal for change
than if you put forward a proposal simply as a personal preference.

Another approach to student motivation and expectations can be
found in Blaxter and Tight (1993). This study investigated the motivation of part-time students, most of whom were mature; you may wish to
investigate whether or not questioning full-time students who have just
left school leads to conclusions which are similar to those cited by
Blaxter and Tight. A study which builds on the authors' results would
make an interesting piece of work, and one which is well worth reporting. In your study you could, first, compare the motivation of part-time
and full-time students and, second, discuss how any differences that are
found between the two modes of study could be addressed within your

department's existing approaches to teaching and assessment. Any differences which cannot be addressed within existing approaches would require you to put forward a proposal as to how all differences might be accommodated within a modified approach to teaching and assessment. A point to remember is that not all differences between the motivation of part-time and full-time students can be addressed through the assessment programme. For example, it would be difficult to see how the assessment programme could make allowances for any demotivation which might arise in some part-time students because they have to attend sessions in the evenings.

Annotated Reading List

Pennington, D (1994) 'Is a competency-based approach suitable for education?', *Higher Education Review*, 27, 1, 69–81.
Although written from a mainly Australian and school-focused perspective, this article provides a very useful critique of the overall purposes of contemporary education and the moves towards competence-based assessment.
Willis, D (1993) 'Learning and assessment: exposing the inconsistencies of theory and practice', *Oxford Review of Education*, 19, 3, 383–402.
This paper adopts a theoretical approach to a consideration of the assumptions and theories which underlie recent developments in student learning, as contained within policy documents, and of the need to ensure a good match between these perspectives and the theory which actually informs assessment practice. The paper presents definitions of many terms relating to learning and assessment, and therefore complements the more practical approach to assessment adopted in this chapter.

References

Blaxter, L and Tight, M (1993) '"I'm only doing it to get a black gown": Dream and reality for adults in part-time higher education', *Journal of Further and Higher Education*, 17, 1, 13–21.
DES and WO (1988) *National Curriculum Task Group on Assessment and Testing. A Report*, London: DES and WO.
Hadley, T and Winn, S (1992) 'Measuring value added at course level: an explanatory study', *Higher Education Review*, 25, 1, 7–30.
Harvey, L and Green, D (1993) 'Defining quality', *Assessment and Evaluation in Higher Education*, 18, 1, 9–34.
Morrison, H, Magennis, P and Carey, L (1995) 'Performance indicators and league tables: a call for standards', *Higher Education Quarterly*, 49, 2, 128–45.
Murphy, P (1988) 'TGAT: a conflict of purpose', *Curriculum*, 9, 3, 152–8.

Chapter 3

Assessment and Quality

In this chapter we look at alternative definitions of quality in assessment. We explore whose interests these serve and how they underpin various purposes of assessment. We look at ways of assessing reliability and validity and systems for monitoring the quality of assessment within and between institutions. We explore the operation and political purposes of performance indicators and consider whether they may distort educational and moral values. Finally, we look at the relationships between assessment objectives and the planning process and consider the implications of each for the quality of student outcomes.

Definitions of Quality in Assessment

The quality of an assessment scheme may be determined in various ways. The scheme may be said to be of high quality because it matches the aims and intentions of the associated programme of study; because it sets rigorous standards, higher than those usually required for a programme at a particular level; because it employs a range of techniques; or because the scheme is subject to extensive quality assurance procedures. Ashcroft and Foreman-Peck (1995) suggest that another criterion by which we should judge an assessment scheme is its coherence across an academic grouping (such as a department) within an institution. Quality demands team work and commitment. A system of assessment may be entirely logical, test all that it should and have many safeguards in place, but still fail in its intentions because those who operate it do not believe in it or feel committed to its success.

There are various ways you might look at the quality of assessment, depending upon whether you take a wide or narrow view of the nature of quality. The narrow view is essentially concerned with quality as expressed through standards. Standards may be seen as an absolute measure: for example, a clearly determined cut-off point for a pass in a particular qualification, or as a relative matter: the difficulty of the assessment or the security of the systems for ensuring comparability of standards between markers.

The definition of standards is essentially a technical matter of reliability and measurement. A wider definition of quality sees this as necessary but insufficient to ensure quality assessment. The validity of assessments is also important. The question of validity is not clear-cut or easy to define. For example, a valid assessment should measure what it purports to and cover the full range of achievement: all the skills, knowledge and attitudes defined as desirable student outcomes at a variety of levels. You might imagine a scheme that fulfils these criteria and that had secure standards and reliable systems for determining them, but nevertheless you would define such a scheme as lacking in quality. For example, the scheme might discriminate against particular student groups, or encourage surface approaches to learning.

Much of the debate about quality during the 1970s and 1980s focused on these wider notions of quality. In the UK, the Council for National Academic Awards (CNAA) and the Further Education Unit (FEU) promoted new ways of looking at quality and encouraged a rigorous examination of the 'hidden curriculum' promoted by different forms of assessment. The view of quality proposed was a developmental one, based on a belief that institutions, departments and individuals were interested in and committed to promoting student learning and in assessing it in a fair and transparent way.

During the late 1980s and early 1990s, a different view of quality developed. This view took quality as something that must be 'policed' and was a matter for comparison. This view requires benchmarks to be established. Reliability is seen as more important than validity. This change resulted in part from real and imagined threats to quality implied by a reducing unit of resource and a changing intake of students, many with non-traditional entry qualifications, and the fear that certain institutions might hide a decline in quality of outcome by diluting standards.

If the definition of quality that you decide to work with stresses comparability of standards, you will have to establish definitions of outcome determined in advance of your research. You may need to assume that observed transactions lead to observable outcomes, that certain of these outcomes are desirable for the students following a programme, and that unanticipated outcomes have less value. You may wish to consider whether the end-point of this kind of definition of quality is extreme commonality of outcome and whether this is a desirable outcome of the competency movement.

You could take the alternative view that diversity is an important factor in educational innovation and development. You may believe that progress comes from challenges to the taken-for-granted ways of doing and conceptualizing things. If you take this view, you might see the increasingly heterogeneous nature of student experience and intakes as an advantage. Students have always had different needs and interests. You might define success as the extent to which these are met. Thus, if you see the aim of the debate about quality in education as improvement, the language of development and review may be more appropriate to your enquiry than that of external quality assessment and audit.

The political right wing across the developed world has an interest in creating a market in education. In order to achieve this, some measures of value for money have to be developed. This can be a fruitful area for investigation. Since assessment frequently results in numerical data, it represents an easy and ready-made performance indicator of quality. You may wish to challenge the belief that quality has to be policed, and the view that academia cannot be trusted to achieve this policing for itself, as a self-fulfilling prophecy. You may wish to investigate whether the use of performance indicators, especially where they are linked to funding, can have a corrupting effect. For instance, you could look at whether institutions are allowing grade inflation to occur where results are linked to funding (see, for instance, Jones and Taylor, 1990). Funders are concerned that academic standards are under threat. By this, they sometimes mean that standards are falling and sometimes that they are becoming less consistent. You might wish to look at the ways that systems for such external assessment have been formalized or elaborated.

In the UK, a course in a college or university may be subject to many forms of quality assessment and audit. Assessment involves looking at the behaviour and actions occurring in the institution to ascertain whether they represent quality in terms of learning, teaching, management and so on. Auditing systems look at whether the institution has itself developed the systems for monitoring quality and ensuring that policies are adhered to. Thus, a quality audit is removed from the direct observation and assessment of behaviour and outcomes.

The quality-related processes that a college or university may be subjected to include:

accreditation – such as that operated by the Teacher Training Agency;
validation – for instance that operated by universities over franchised
    courses within further education colleges;

inspection – for example, that operated by OFSTED;

quality audit – for instance, that operated by the Higher Education Quality Council;

quality assessment – such as the assessments of quality and value for money operated by the Higher and Further Education Funding Councils;

internal course review – sometimes including external members in the review panel;

external examiners and moderators;

institutional self-assessment;

performance indicators determined from time to time by the relevant Secretary of State.

Each of the various forms of quality assessment may have their own internal coherence and some validity, but their cumulative impact on student experience and the extent to which they relate to the interests and needs of students have seldom been investigated.

RESEARCH TASK. INVESTIGATING THE NATURE OF EVIDENCE IN QUALITY AUDIT AND ASSESSMENT

Look at various reports about a course that has been subject to multiple forms of quality audit and assessment. In each report, note the extent to which:

student views on the quality of their learning are directly sought and reported;

an assessment of the quality of student learning is derived from direct observation of student behaviour;

statements about quality appear to be based on an indirectly observed assessment of student learning;

an assessment of the quality of student learning is derived from an analysis of course processes.

(Look at Ashcroft, Jones and Siraj-Blatchford, 1996, for ways of deconstructing texts.)

Discuss with an experienced colleague your interpretation of various statements within the reports and how you determined that they should appear in one category rather than another.

Use your study as the basis for an exploration of the extent to which quality assessment/auditing agencies' claims that their activities are directed at improving student learning can be supported by the reported data underpinning their quality assessments.

Consider the evidence reported to support the reliability and validity of assessments of the quality of student learning contained in the reports.

Audiences for Quality

Quality issues in education are defined in part by the interests of the stakeholders in the education process, such as funders, students, lecturers, managers, employers and the community (see Chapter 2). You could look at the ways that the vested interests of each of these groups of people are reflected in particular definitions of quality, the impact of each set of concerns on assessment issues and the ways that quality assessment is actualized.

You might decide to investigate whether the concerns of the stakeholders in education are compatible. For instance, academic study at higher levels requires people who can see things in new ways and who can look critically at taken-for-granted assumptions about the way things are: in other words, people who have the courage, and the ability, to think and express difficult and unconventional thoughts. You could look at the extent to which lecturers see study at lower levels as a preparation for higher-level achievements. Alternatively, you might investigate whether they use the assessment scheme to reward those who are able to analyse situations in some depth and have developed the capability of independent and original thought.

Employers, on the other hand, may be more interested in people who will make 'good' employees. You could explore their definitions of successful outcomes: for instance, whether they see them in terms of the extent to which the student is equipped with the skills to work as part of a team, the discipline to work effectively against set targets and the willingness to internalize and further the organizational culture and ethos. In other words, whether they are interested in conformity and compliance, rather than originality.

The student may wish to develop a set of skills that equips her or him for a whole life: positive participation in employment, leisure, culture and, perhaps, unemployment. You could investigate whether a particular assessment scheme helps them to develop those skills: for instance, the ability to analyse the politics of the workplace, so as to know when to 'leave the sinking ship'; knowledge and skills in sports, cultural pursuits or the arts so as to enjoy a satisfying leisure and social life; and the interpersonal skills to manoeuvre for personal and social advantage.

You might find that each of the stakeholders in education has multiple needs and interests that are hard to reconcile within a single definition of quality in assessment. You could look at the problems in designing programmes and criteria for assessment to achieve and test the various sets of objectives of each of the stakeholders. For instance, you might find that employers are particularly interested in summative assessments that enable reliable comparisons between individuals at the stage when they are selecting between candidates for employment: in other words, a single numerical mark. On the other hand, they might also wish for programmes of study that cover and assess a broad range of knowledge and competence. They might need employees with skills in team working, in communication, in analysis and so on (see Chapter 2). These may be best assessed in ways that result in more complex statements of attainment than a simple end grade.

RESEARCH TASK. EXPLORING THE FEATURES OF A 'GOOD' ASSESSMENT SCHEME

Set up group interviews with each of:

a group of employers;
a group of students;
a group of institutional managers; and
a group of lecturers.

The members of the group should have an interest in a particular programme. (See Ashcroft, Bigger and Coates (1996) for details of the group focus technique – one method of obtaining data from a homogeneous group.)

Ask each member of each group to list the features of a 'good' assessment scheme. Use nominal group technique to create a composite list of the features suggested by the members of each group and to get each group to rank the list in order of importance. (See Ashcroft and Foreman-Peck, 1994, pp.174–5 for an outline of how to operate this technique.)

Use the results of this group analysis as a starting point for an investigation into definitions of quality in assessment held by some of the various stake-holders in education.

Quality Assurance Systems and Assessment

There are two main ways of looking at quality issues in assessment: through quality audit and through quality assessment. In the UK, the Higher Education Quality Council (HEQC) is an example of a quality audit system. The Higher Education Funding Council (HEFC) sends in inspectors to look at teaching, learning outcomes and assessment directly: an example of a quality assessment system.

Each system can be operated through insider or peer review, or through outsider monitoring. Thus, the HEQC operates as a users' club, with auditors from other institutions who have agreed to abide by certain rules. The auditors' role is to conduct an enquiry to find out whether the institution is abiding by the rules it has set for itself. You might wish to explore whether, in reality, auditors will look for certain features that they believe are commonly accepted as good practice in assessment. You might investigate whether they look for a rigorous system for the appointment of external examiners and for ensuring that the examiners' views are taken into account or whether they seek some assurance that efforts are made to ensure that assessments are reliable and free from personal bias. Quality audit should be primarily about the bureaucratic framework within which assessment operates, rather than the actuality of its practice. In assessing the validity of audit judgements, you will need to bear in mind that these are seen in terms of the security against bias contained within the system.

RESEARCH TASK. ANALYSING IMPLICIT AND EXPLICIT CRITERIA FOR JUDGING AN ASSESSMENT SYSTEM

Find out what systems exist for auditing assessment within your institution. Look at the documentation produced by the system: for example, committee minutes, policy documents, course leader reports, etc. List the explicit and implicit criteria by which the quality of an assessment system is judged, for example:

assessment across the institution should be on the basis of commonly accepted principles;
students should be informed in advance about the assessments they will experience within their programme of study.

Compare the criteria used for judgements about the quality of assessment systems within your institution against those implied by reports from other institutions (eg, HEQC reports). Are they the same? Should they be the same?
Discuss your judgements with an experienced institutional manager.
Use this analysis as the starting point for an enquiry into the nature of quality implied by the process of quality audit. You could use this as a springboard for a discussion of the interests served by the focus on bureaucracy within the process of audit.

Institutions in the UK seem to be attracted to the process of quality audit, since it protects them from an independent inspection system that might have imposed its own objectives for higher education. Quality audit also enables institutions to define quality in ways that suit their particular interests. Government, as the funding agency, is less happy with this system. It wants to be able to compare and rate institutional quality against 'objective' criteria, in order to ascertain and compare the value for money provided by different institutions. The tradition of autonomy within British universities and their influence within political circles requires Funding Councils to compromise, and has led to a system of peer inspection, moderated by professional inspectors, that looks at actual practice, but which sets this practice against institutional and departmental self-assessment and internally derived objectives.

Further education institutions have no such tradition of autonomy and in England the Further Education Funding Council (FEFC) has been able to impose a more fully developed system of external assessment. This quality assessment generally operates at departmental level. It is overtly judgemental in approach, involving outside inspectors' judgements of performance. FEFC has its own criteria for determining quality in assessment and external assessors are guided firmly in the judgements they should make according to various quality indicators.

Quality assessment involves the examination of actual practice, rather than merely looking at systems. You could explore the judgements that are made about the validity of assessment schemes. For instance, whether instruments are effective in assessing the aims and objectives of programmes, whether they are set at an appropriate level, and whether there is an appropriate variety of assessment methods to allow students to demonstrate a variety of achievement. Alternatively, you could look at whether the effectiveness and the appropriateness of assessments themselves are judged, rather than just their reliability (see Chapter 4 for more details).

Some other systems for quality assurance have been around for a long time. Perhaps the most common involves monitoring the quality of tutor assessment by a group of peers, usually in the form of a committee set up to oversee the quality assurance system within the institution and to recommend changes to it. You could investigate the ways that the committee systems in various institutions operate. For example, some may examine the extent of compliance with institutional policies by those operating assessment systems, perhaps by looking at evidence within course reports and students' evaluation. On the other hand, some institutions may be satisfied with reassurance from the managers of assessment about the extent of policy compliance.

Most assessment systems rely on sub-systems to ensure the quality, and especially the reliability, of assessments. One of the most widely used checks for reliability within an assessment system is the use of external assessors, who look at all, or a sample of, assessed work and attest to the fairness, comparability and, sometimes, appropriateness of the marking process.

In UK universities, the external examiner system has been under discussion for some time. You might explore the effectiveness of this system in achieving its main objectives: to ensure inter-institutional comparability of standards, the fair treatment of students and, within some institutions, the promotion of good practice in assessment. You may wish to consider whether the system has particular weaknesses. For instance, you might look at the need for national monitoring of and training for external examiners. External examiners generally operate in no more than three institutions. You might assess the evidence that their ability to comment on comparability of standards between institutions is greater, and their comments on assessment practices or fairness to students is more valid, than those of the internal examiners. You could look at those situations where pairs or small groups of departments exchange examiners in order to enquire into the opportunities for small-scale corruption: for example, whether examiners in such circumstances are more inclined to provide positive reports than examiners operating in institutions where such reciprocal arrangements are not allowed.

You might investigate other factors that influence the quality of the external examiner system within an institution. You could look at whether individuals feel that they need to receive training or other preparation for the role and the effects of such preparation. You might also explore the extent to which external assessors rely on detailed briefing and whether examiners know the intention behind each assessment, the criteria by which student achievements are to be judged and the extent to which contextual factors may be taken into account (for instance in work-based learning). In addition, you could look at examination regulations and how these are communicated to examiners: for instance, the rules for changing, adding or combining marks, and those governing compensation or progression.

The inter-institutional reliability of the external examiner system may be threatened by a range of factors. You might explore the variation in institutional and subject practices in the nature and scope of the duties of external examiners (see the research task below for some of the factors that may vary between institutions or departments). Within the UK, there is no national requirement for external examiners to comment on the quality and scope of candidates' work, the standards achieved, the coverage of the course by the assessment scheme, the quality of work within particular mark bands, the management of the assessment process, or examination regulations, procedures and methods. You could investigate the extent to which examiners actually do so, and the usefulness of such comments as perceived by each of those involved in the assessment and quality assurance process.

The external examiner system depends upon the notion that the reliability of assessment is appropriately regulated by an autonomous institution. Where this assumption is not made, for instance in much of further education within the UK, a much more closely defined moderation role may be imposed across substantial parts of the system. An example of this is the training of examiners and the extensive moderation process within the National Vocational Qualification (NVQ) system. You could investigate the costs and benefits of such training and moderation experienced by the educational institution.

RESEARCH TASK. INVESTIGATING EXTERNAL EXAMINER SYSTEMS

Investigate the external examiner systems within two or more institutions, *or* two or more subject departments within the same institution.

Use documents sent to external examiners, institutional quality assurance documents, registry guidelines, course documents and external examiners' reports to analyse some of the following:

the information routinely sent to examiners;
the written ground rules to which the examiners are expected to conform;
the scope for an examination board to overrule an examiner's recommendation;
the scope of the examiners' reports.

You might also examine the scope of external examiners' duties in relation to:

visiting the institution;
discussion with the teaching/marking team;
resolving disagreements between internal markers;
viva voce examinations;
project work;
work assessed through live presentations;
the assessment of professional competence;

---

the aggregation of examination and other marks;
student performance judged in practical situations.

You could investigate the scope of the examiners in relation to course development and review; for example advising on:

the marking scheme;
the form of assessments;
regulations and procedures;
teaching and learning methods;
the syllabus.

Find out whether external examiners in the different contexts see all, any, or a fixed proportion, of the following:

examination papers before publication;
coursework assignments before publication;
student work given borderline, top or failing marks;
candidates' work where there are mitigating circumstances;
candidates' work where there are irregularities.

Discuss your preliminary interpretations and conclusions with some internal and external examiners from the institutions/departments you have been investigating.

Use the results of your analysis as the basis of a discursive paper on the consistency of aims and/or practice within the external examiner system. Compare your analysis with the exposition of the issues and problems posed by the external examination system in Silver (1993).

Issues of Reliability and Validity in Assessment

Brown and Knight (1994) give a good description of the operation of validity and reliability in assessment; we also include more details in Chapter 4. Reliability relates to the consistency of measurement or measurements. You may wish to investigate various aspects of this consistency, such as inter-marker agreement, the agreement between instruments that purport to measure the same aspect of a course (for instance, examinations and essays covering understanding of basic concepts), or agreements between the same measure (test–retest procedures).

Much institutional energy has gone into ensuring reliability of assessment in recent years. For example, in the UK, senior posts have been created in many colleges and universities to oversee academic standards, and institutions have created policy documents in anticipation of inspection and audit visits. You may wish to consider whether this has sometimes been at the expense of concern for the validity of assessment and whether, in any case, the expectation that one can reliably assess students' educational achievement may be false. Education changes people, so test–retest procedures may be an inappropriate measure of reliability. The assessment of higher level of achievement almost invariably relies on judgements. You may need to think about whether these can be 'right', but still subjective.

You may feel that validity – the question of whether you have measured what you have set out to measure – is a more pertinent issue. The validity question allows you to explore changes and developments in students' attitudes, initiative, analysis and other processes that may not result in directly observable behaviour. Brown and Knight (1994) point out that reliability generally demands that assessment occurs in standardized settings, but validity may require assessment within real life and variable settings, such as actual workplaces. Assessments that are high on reliability can be low on validity, and vice versa.

Both reliability and validity pose questions about the nature of assessment evidence: the sufficiency of the claims made of assessment and the extent to which claims are met. In thinking about validity, you may decide also to look at whether assessment measures have desirable effects.

Ridgeway (1992) discusses the political context of assessment and its effect on the reliability and validity of assessments. Astute educationalists recognize that all assessment instruments have in-built error, but that the nature of this error varies between instruments. Ridgeway sees the educational, moral, philosophical and political values that underpin assessment as basic to its quality. Without a notion of educational and moral defensibility, there are opportunities for corruption. The operation of the 'corruption coefficient' – the extent to which scores can be raised (or lowered) without changes in teaching or learning, by subtly adjusting assessment tasks, processes or context – could make an interesting area of enquiry.

RESEARCH TASK. ANALYSING IMPLICIT CRITERIA USED IN MARKING

Look at a range of markers' comments on essays or other course work at a particular level. Analyse the criteria implied by each marker's comments, for example:

depth of knowledge;
breadth of sources quoted;
level of analysis;
use of personal knowledge or experience;
appropriateness of response;
clarity of argument;
originality of thought;
grasp of underpinning theory;
clarity of structure;
use of references;
use of grammar;
spelling;
attractiveness of presentation.

(See Ashcroft, Jones and Siraj-Blatchford, 1996, for ways of establishing emerging data categories.)

Discuss and compare your analysis and categorization of certain of the comments with those of the original markers.

Obtain the original markers' permission to make an assessment of the priority given to each of these factors by different markers as indicated by their written comments. In what ways do these comments relate to the assessment criteria and the aims and objectives of the course or unit covered?

You might use your results as a starting point for various kinds of investigation. For instance, you could analyse other marked papers from various institutions or from different subject areas (you could use information technology to help you – see Bennett et al., 1996, for ways of doing this), as the basis of a discursive paper on:

the appropriateness of second marking systems as an indicator of
 reliability of assessments, or
the level of agreement among markers as to the criteria implicitly valued
 as indicators of highly and/or lowly assessed achievement (see Chapter
 4).

Alternatively, you might develop an intervention study into, for instance, the effectiveness of the second marking system, as against staff training, for safeguarding reliability in assessment.

Performance Indicators, Assessment and Monitoring

Performance indicators are the means by which funders and others can compare institutional inputs (for instance, staff and capital costs) with outputs (for instance, students' final grades and the career paths of graduates) in order to assess performance. A wide range of factors have been suggested as suitable for assessing the performance of educational institutions and departments. Many of these can be measured fairly precisely. Examples include drop-out rates of students on courses, levels and types of qualifications achieved, the first destination of students after completing the programme and the average unit of funding. Each of these may be used as a bureaucratic measure of how well an institution is doing and may inform funding.

The growth in popularity of performance indicators among funders may have resulted from an increasing suspicion amongst them as to the responsiveness of institutions to the economic needs of society. It also reflects the dilemmas posed by the desire to increase the average level of qualification and achievement of the workforce, coupled with the feeling that post-compulsory education is too reliant on public funds. In addition, governments are increasingly eager to target their funding of institutions and to require them to become more cost-conscious. Educational and non-educational performance indicators represent ways of influencing institutional policy and behaviour along the desired lines.

You may decide to explore the extent to which the simplicity of performance indicators can capture education as a complex activity, involving multiple goals, factors and benefits. For example, you may find that some of these, such as social and cultural benefits, are diffuse and difficult to measure and that others are subject to intra-student and intra-institutional variables that influence outcomes but say nothing about quality as defined by particular interest groups.

Jones and Taylor (1990) describe the problems mentioned above in some detail, especially as they relate to assessment. Among the assessment-related performance indicators that may be used to assess the quality of education are the numbers of students achieving a particular degree class or level of qualification. In the UK, the number of students in different universities achieving higher grades in undergraduate degrees (first class and 2:1 honours degrees) varies considerably. Interestingly, although the numbers in this category are rising in most universities, the differences between particular universities appear to be fairly consistent over time. If you have access to them, you could use statistical data to explore the reasons for this. For instance, consistency in the academic ability of the students on intake; the proportion of students living on campus or at home; or the proportion of students who are working in a language other than their mother tongue. You might also look at the effect of the institutional subject mix, the marking traditions of the institution, and the proportion of students on courses achieving the highest level of award. You might consider which of these factors actually relate to institutional or departmental quality.

Another measure that may be used by funders to assess the quality of provision within an institution is the first destination of students: the proportion going on to employment and further education. Again, Jones and Taylor (op cit) describe a range of factors that might affect the institutional or departmental score on such a measure, which cause difficulties in making inferences about quality from them. You could look at the factors that lead to students leaving or remaining in the institution: for instance, some unsuccessful students may continue study to retake the qualification to remediate their learning problems, and some very successful students may wish to study for higher-level qualifications. Again, you could consider whether these kinds of student outcomes can really measure the quality of the education that the students experience.

There may also be a variety of non-educational features of the university or college that influence the employment prospects of its students. For instance, in the UK, graduates of some universities are more attractive to employers and some institutions offer a higher proportion of vocationally-oriented courses. The effects of employer attitudes on the first destination of students might be a fruitful area of investigation: you might explore employer attitudes to students from different kinds of institution.

You might also consider the effect of the social class of students, the network of contacts supplied by their parents and the location and level of unemployment surrounding the university or college on the ease with which graduates find employment. You could look at the influence of the age and sex of students: for instance, whether mature female students tend to have restricted employment opportunities compared with younger students, because they need to find employment close to home.

Jones and Taylor (op cit) also describe the complex operation of completion rates of students as a performance indicator. Raw data hide great differences in student experience and the value for money provided by institutions. Thus, an institution that concentrates its drop-out from courses in the first year may be said to be performing better than one with a lower drop-out rate, but where this happens later in the course. You could investigate this area: for instance, whether certain groups on courses at various levels (for example, men, people from deprived and non-traditional backgrounds, people living at home and younger students) are particularly prone to non-completion. The subject disciplines that students study may make a difference. You could look at whether scientific and non-vocational courses have similar rates as vocational courses and whether the same factors operate at different levels within the educational system. (In doing this you will have to take care that the variables do not get confounded: for example, in the UK, engineering in some 'old' universities is academic and non-professional in its focus.) You might also explore the effects of the length of courses or the effect of accelerated courses on student drop-out rates.

Despite the problems, performance indicators are still used as a measure of quality. Intellectual arguments and the power of institutions have not been well used to resist this trend. As recently as 1985, a report commissioned by the Committee of Vice-Chancellors and Principals (Jarratt, 1985) suggested that graduation rates, degree classification, success rates and the acceptability of graduates to employers would be valid performance indicators.

Performance indicators, as soon as they are linked to funding, can have a distorting effect on institutional or departmental policy. You could explore the public pronouncements of institutional managers before and after such linkage occurs. You might interview the authors of some of these pronouncements, in order to discover the extent to which managers are influenced by the worry that their institution may be penalized if they are not seen to be playing the game wholeheartedly. If academia is one of the bulwarks of a free society, any muzzling of dissent should be a matter of concern.

You could investigate whether performance indicators, linked to funding, applied in the context of assessment, seem to pose a real threat to integrity, validity and reliability. For example, you could explore whether, once completion rates are used as a measure of performance, fewer students are awarded a fail grade. You might interview course leaders to find out whether some students are discouraged from leaving courses for which they may be unsuited because of funding considerations. You might look at the effect on the movement towards credit accumulation and transfer schemes between institutions, and in particular whether there is any attempt to restrict student mobility and to keep students within the institution or department. For example, it could be interesting to find out whether departments within institutions operating modular programmes are tending to make their course more specialized, with a larger compulsory core of modules, in order to ensure that students must take most modules within a particular department and to make transfer to other departments more difficult.

Where the average grade achieved by students at the end of their course is introduced as a measure of performance, there may be an effect on the entry standard. You might wish to look at whether performance indicators linked to funding perpetuate and increase inequalities in society at the institutional level (perhaps by rewarding those that exist in prosperous neighbourhoods) and the individual student level (for instance, by denying socially deprived, 'risky' or non-traditional students access to education). You might also look at the numbers of students completing as a proportion of those starting the course. For instance, more students might be failed at the early stages so that only the 'good' ones take final examinations. If employment rates are introduced as a measure of performance, you might interview teaching staff to find out if formative assessment reports, references and student profiles paint a rosier picture of average student achievement.

Relationships Between Assessment Outcomes, Planning and Processes

An interesting area of investigation is the relationship between the purposes of assessment, their forms and the way that they operate in practice (see Chapter 2). One way you can look at this is to measure the extent to which assessments appear to be congruent with the aims and purposes of a particular programme of learning from the point of view of the various parties to the assessment process.

Clarity about the purposes of assessment is an area worthy of enquiry. You might document discussion during the planning stage of the development of a number of programmes to find out whether various definitions of quality in assessment are routinely built in at this stage. For example, Atkins *et al.* (1993) suggest that assessment processes should represent educational experiences of value in their own right. They should provide a foundation for other knowledge creation, as well as for vocational life. These purposes require balance between them. For instance, they underpin the debate about the balance between assessment of competence and the assessment of personal and professional understanding. You could analyse whether these considerations feature in the discussion or whether there is a tendency to see certain forms of assessment as beneficial in themselves. Within programme development, you might look at whether assessment has driven teaching and learning processes, or whether particular definitions of quality in teaching and learning have determined the assessment process.

Programmes based on the development of competence may provide fruitful areas for such investigation. You could look at the definitions of competence operating within such programmes. Operational competence is an outcome-focused notion that has become a defining criterion for quality in large sectors of education, replacing academic competence as the dominant assessment focus. It is closely related to the skills needed in particular operational areas (such as certain occupations), as opposed to academic competence, which relates to the knowledge and skills needed to operate successfully within a particular discipline. Barnett (1994) argues that educational quality demands that we go beyond competence (both operational and academic) as a model for quality in education. Competence is sometimes defined in terms of outcomes concerned with tackling problems. It may be more appropriate for higher-level education to address understanding and thinking about problems. You could explore whether transformational solutions, requiring problems to be conceptualized in new ways, are discouraged as Barnett implies, if tackling is the dominant mode of assessment.

Barnett points out that real independence of mind may not be valued by the competency movement. You could explore his notion that assessment based on competence encourages reproduction: whether prestated criteria can take account of new ideas or of people who are capable of bringing new processes into existence and whether, where competence is defined pragmatically, it is closed to multiple definition. It might be interesting to look at whether in practice competence schemes stress propositions and outcomes at the expense of the ability to argue and whether they do focus on experience to the exclusion of reflection on learning. The values that underpin competence schemes are often economic. You may want to consider whether these work against wider definitions of the 'common good' and are bounded by organizational and subject norms, rather than the limits imposed by logical discourse. You may find that practical effectiveness is valued at the expense of practical understanding and that competence is a limited measure of quality in assessment. On the other hand, you may find that such schemes open doors for some students to the broader world of education and new ways of thinking.

RESEARCH TASK. ANALYSING THE MATCH BETWEEN CRITERIA
FOR ASSESSMENT AND LEARNING OBJECTIVES

The categories of abilities and attitudes of individual students listed below
are taken from Atkins et al (1993). List those abilities and attitudes below that
you think are relevant for people training for a broad area of work (eg,
working with children):

Cognitive learning:
verbal skills, eg, listening, reading, writing;
quantitative skills, eg, statistical data analysis;
substantive knowledge, eg, cultural heritage or subject knowledge;
rationality, eg, logical thinking, analysis and synthesis;
intellectual perspective, eg, appreciation of cultural diversity;
aesthetic sensitivity, eg, knowledge or responsiveness to the arts;
creativity, eg, imagination and originality in formulating hypotheses, ideas
   or works of art;
intellectual integrity, eg, truthfulness, conscientiousness and accuracy in
   enquiry;
lifelong learning, eg, awareness of the value of education, ability to learn
   independently, ability to locate information.

Emotional and moral development:
self-awareness, eg, knowledge of strengths and weaknesses;
psychological well-being, eg, sensitivity and ability to cope with deep
   feeling, self-confidence, ability to deal with life's difficulties;
human understanding, eg, capacity for empathy, compassion and respect
   for others, ability to cooperate;
values and morals, eg, awareness of moral issues and traditions, personal
   set of moral principles;
religion, eg, awareness and respect for varieties of religious thought;

Practical competence:
traits of value in practical affairs generally, eg, ability to apply knowledge
   and negotiate, motivation, initiative, resourcefulness;
leadership, eg, capacity to assume authority and to seek advice;
citizenship, eg, commitment to democracy, knowledge of major systems
   of government, awareness of social issues;
work and careers, eg, awareness of needs of the workplace, knowledge
   and ability to make sound career decisions, employability skills;
family life, eg, personal qualities relevant to family life;
leisure, eg, appropriate balance between work and leisure;
health, eg, understanding basic principles of physical and mental health,
   participation in physical recreation.

Check and refine your list with practitioners actually working in the occupational area.

Analyse which of these abilities and attitudes in your final list are actually assessed in a variety of competence-based and other programmes for people training for the occupational area under study.

Discuss the preliminary results of this enquiry and your interpretation of them with groups of staff and students working within the programmes.

Use your analysis as the starting point for an investigation into the range of competence and knowledge considered valid in programmes that include particular models of assessment.

You might go on to:

- compare them with those perceived as valuable among practitioners within the field and among educationalists;
- discuss the balance and/or comparability between vocationally-oriented assessment and educationally-oriented assessment within training for a particular work area.

Annotated Reading List

Ashcroft, K and Foreman-Peck, L (1995) *The Lecturer's Guide to Quality and Standards in Colleges and Universities*, London: Falmer Press.
This book provides user-friendly definitions of quality in educational practice. There is a chapter that looks in particular at quality issues in assessment.

Atkins, MJ, Beatie, J and Dockrell, WB (1993) *Assessment Issues in Higher Education*, London: Employment Department Development Group.
A report that looks at assessment in relation to the various purposes of education and the implications of these purposes for practice.

Burgess, R and Lee, B (1989) *Good Practice in Assessment: Criteria and procedures for CNAA Undergraduate Courses*, London: CNAA.
A clear set of guidelines for recognizing good practice in aspects of assessment.

Dochy, F, Segers, M and Wijnen, W (eds) (1990) *Management Information and Performance Indicators in Higher Education: An international issue*, Assen/Maastricht: Van Gorcum.
A collection of examples of the ways quality assessment is approached, especially the form, role and function of performance indicators.

Doherty, GD (1994) *Developing Quality Systems in Education*, London: Routledge.
An edited collection of case studies and reflections on the application of Total Quality Management to education.

Ellis, R (1993) *Quality Assurance for University Teaching*, Buckingham: SRHE/Open University Press.
A basic, edited text, covering quality assurance, definitions of quality and some outlines of ways of developing quality.

Further Education Unit (1994) *Examining Assessment*, London: FEU.
An analysis of the role of assessment in colleges. It includes a descriptive account of the assessment requirements of various examining bodies in the UK.

Her Majesty's Inspectorate/Office for Standards in Education *Standards in Education*, London: HMSO/DfE.

Each year in the UK, the chief inspector comments upon the state of the educational system. The resulting reports are a good source for mapping the changing priorities and criteria for quality.

Higher Education Quality Council (1994) *A Briefing Paper from the Higher Education Quality Council: A checklist for quality audit systems*, London: HEQC.

A very short summary of aspects that should be included within a quality control system.

Knight, P (ed.) (1993) *The Audit of Teaching Quality*, Birmingham: Standing Conference on Educational Development.

A collection of research studies and literature reviews looking at various aspects of quality audit and assessment.

Race, P (1993) *Never Mind the Teaching, Feel the Learning*, Birmingham: Staff and Educational Development Association.

This short, easy to read book has chapters on competence-based assessment, judging quality in assessment and BS 5750 for assessment.

Silver, H (1993) *External Examiners: Changing roles?*, London: CNAA.

The report of a project looking at the structures and roles of examination boards and the preparation and expectations of external examiners, especially in relation to comparability of standards and the promotion of quality.

References

Ashcroft, K and Foreman-Peck, L (1994) *Managing Teaching and Learning in Further and Higher Education*, London: Falmer Press.

Ashcroft, K and Foreman-Peck, L (1995) *The Lecturer's Guide to Quality and Standards in Colleges and Universities*, London: Falmer Press.

Ashcroft, K, Bigger, S and Coates, D (1996) *Researching into Equal Opportunities in Colleges and Universities*, London: Kogan Page.

Ashcroft, K, Jones, M and Siraj-Blatchford, J (1996) *Researching into Student Learning and Support in Colleges and Universities*, London: Kogan Page.

Atkins, MJ, Beatie, J and Dockrell, WB (1993) *Assessment Issues in Higher Education*, London: Employment Department Development Group.

Barnett, R (1994) *The Limits of Competence: Knowledge, higher education and society*, Buckingham: SHRE/Open University Press.

Brown, S and Knight, P (1994) *Assessing Learners in Higher Education*, London: Kogan Page.

Bennett, C, Higgins, C and Foreman-Peck, L (1996) *Researching into Teaching Methods in Colleges and Universities*, London: Kogan Page.

Jarratt, A (1985) *Report of the Steering Committee for Efficiency Studies in Universities*, London: Committee of Vice-Chancellors and Principals.

Jones, J and Taylor, J (1990) *Performance Indicators in Higher Education*, Buckingham: SRHE/Open University Press.

Ridgeway, J (1992) *The Assessment of Teaching Quality*, Lancaster: Faculty of Social Science, Lancaster University.

Silver, H (1993) *External Examiners: Changing roles?*, London: CNAA.

Chapter 4

Methods of Assessment

In Chapter 2 we reviewed some of the main purposes of assessment. One purpose discussed was premised on the view that assessment was the means through which the various stakeholders – students, potential employers, funding agencies, etc – were informed of the progress and achievements of students, collectively as well as individually, as measured against the various course outcomes, implicit as well as explicit. Explicit outcomes of a course are often stated in terms of student learning: what the successful student should be expected to know, understand or be able to do at the end of a component or course. These outcomes may be expressed rather generally – aims and objectives – or by statements which encompass greater specificity, for example, criterion statements or descriptions in terms of a particular competence.

When discussing learning outcomes it is sometimes helpful to be able to distinguish between:

- the outcome itself;
- how the outcome is to be measured (for example, a percentage, a grade, pass/fail);
- the form in which the result is to be communicated to students, etc;
- how outcome measures are combined across the various other elements of the course so as to produce a final grade or other measure of award;
- how all of this information is communicated to students and other people with an interest in the progress of students, either individually or collectively.

In this chapter we will discuss only the first two of these points, namely the nature of the course outcomes and how the expected outcomes are to be measured.

Validity and Reliability in Relation to Methods of Assessment

Acceptance of the point that any assessment programme needs be designed in such a way as to measure student learning leads on to perhaps two obvious, but nevertheless important, conclusions: first, that the methods of assessment employed must enable measures to be made of those learning outcomes, and second, that these measures should be both *reliable* and *valid*. Any attempt to provide an adequate explanation of the meaning of the terms 'reliability' and 'validity' is likely to be complex, especially when that explanation is considered within educational settings, a point you will have no doubt discovered when reading Chapter 3. If you are interested and wish to know more, then you might consult a textbook on assessment and testing, for example Frith and Macintosh (1984). Briefly, and in the context of this chapter, reliability refers to the extent to which an assignment when given to a student on different occasions produces the same outcome measure (grade, mark, etc) of the assessment criteria being applied. The question to ask yourself is, would your students obtain the same assessment on one of your tests if that test was administered to them on different occasions and marked by different people? Clearly, not a question that can be answered easily; you might expect students to have learnt something from doing the test and therefore even if the test was highly reliable you might still expect them to do better the second time around. However, work that has been done in this area indicates that many methods of assessment (essays, examination, for example) produce quite unreliable measures of the assessment criteria they are supposed to be measuring.

Validity, on the other hand, refers to the extent to which an assignment actually measures what it is intended to measure and, as such, is a concept which is much easier to investigate, a point which we shall make use of during this chapter.

The following questions illustrate the sorts of issues which you need to give some thought to when considering matters relating to validity:

- Is the outcome of a written assignment which asks students to describe how they would perform a practical task a valid measure of how well, let alone whether or not a particular student can actually perform that task?
- Do the outcomes of the same practical task, this time actually undertaken cooperatively on a single occasion by a group of six students, constitute a valid measure of whether or not each individual student can undertake that task by her or himself?

Problematic as answers to questions such as these are, the issue becomes much more complex when validity is considered alongside reliability. Often, the two concepts appear to act as if they were in opposition to one another; assignments that have high validity are often associated with low reliability, and vice versa. However, in the context of this book, and as we mentioned in Chapter 3, reliability is considered to be of less significance than validity. For a better understanding of both concepts please refer to Frith and Macintosh (1984) and to some of the publications mentioned at the back of this book.

If we go back about 25 years in the case of further education in the UK but less than 10 years in the case of higher education, the focus for quality was academic excellence as measured by students' written work, especially that produced during end of course examinations. In secondary schools in England and Wales, as in many other countries, courses for most pupils were designed around the requirements of fixed, externally set, academic syllabuses. This situation persisted even though these syllabuses were generally acknowledged to be appropriate for only the most academically able pupils (about 20 per cent of the age cohort in England). Assessment was determined also in the main by written examinations taken at the end of two years of study: in a number of subjects little attention was paid to either coursework or the notion of continuous assessment. In the UK, success in these courses, and usually only these courses, was a necessary prerequisite to higher education and, to a lesser extent, further education. In addition, up until fairly recently secondary schools were the main access routes into full-time further and higher education courses. Thus, in terms of assessment, student progress could be seen as a seamless academic web of written summative assessments, extending from school to undergraduate and through to postgraduate study.

Leaving aside the issue of whether the assessment of knowledge and understanding through written work alone is a valid or even reliable way to assess students' overall development, the expansion of post-compulsory education in Britain, and in particular higher education, has seen for the first time a new kind of student enter this phase of education in significant numbers. This change has come about in part because of developments that have taken place in schools in respect of styles and forms of teaching, learning and assessment. Significant amongst these changes has been the introduction of the General Certificate of Secondary Education (GCSE) at 16 with its emphasis on coursework and participative styles of learning, and a redefinition of the purpose and focus of 16-plus education, for example, the introduction of General

National Vocational Qualifications (GNVQs) – the so-called vocational Advanced Level GCE – and National Vocational Qualifications. The effects of these developments pre-18 are beginning to be felt by universities and colleges: some potential students who are now applying to them (successfully) have experienced an education in school which has been participative and practical as well as theoretical, and not, as in the past, mainly passive and theoretical. In other words, these students have been successful on courses which have laid emphasis on assessment through both 'doing' and 'writing'. This type of student, quite naturally, is looking to further and higher education to provide courses which reflect, through the assessment programme, this mix of practical and theoretical work.

The move towards more participative and practical styles of teaching and learning has been a long time coming. Not everyone in the UK has welcomed the changes that this move brought about. A significant obstacle in the route towards a general acceptance and widespread introduction of courses in which 'application of theory through practical work' plays an important part, has been a desire on the part of the UK government to retain traditional *academic* school-leaving examinations at 18 as the 'gold standard' of excellence. A consequence has been the difficulty of setting up alongside 'A' levels any courses that are seen as being different in emphasis, for example practical rather than purely academic, but which lead to qualifications of equivalent standing. The appearance in schools and colleges of courses leading to GNVQ qualifications could be conceived as a softening of this position.

Variety in Assessment

Variety within an assessment programme is an idea which underpins the concepts of reliability and validity. One important result to arise out of the work of the Assessment of Performance Unit (APU), admittedly in primary and secondary schools, was a realization that the marks awarded were very much dependent on the way the tasks were set; for example, whether the tasks involved writing, drawing or practical work. What is significant about the APU work is the fact that although the tasks may be different each one was meant to be assessing common learning outcomes (Qualter, 1988). This implies that variety of assessment methods – essays, examinations, practical work presentations, project work, and so on – is essential if learning outcomes are to be reported with any degree of confidence. On the other hand, if it is accepted that a main purpose of assessment is to measure in a reliable and valid way the learning outcomes of individual students it does not necessarily follow that *every* assignment must attempt to measure *every* intended outcome, but rather that assignments collectively must do so.

RESEARCH TASK. MAPPING TASKS AGAINST MODES AND METHODS OF ASSESSMENT

Choose a course which you and several close colleagues teach on.

Compile a portfolio of all the different assessment tasks which are given to students at some stage during their course. Don't forget to include the informal tasks that students do as part of their ongoing learning as well as the more formal assignments which contribute to either an intermediate or final award.

Construct a grid with the tasks listed on the vertical axis set against the mode of assessment on the horizontal axis. Now complete the grid, mapping the task onto the way(s) in which it is assessed. The grid, in outline form, may start to look like this:

Task/Mode	practical	written	presentation	work place	visit
Individual task	✓				
Essay		✓			✓
Seen examination		✓			
Group project	✓		✓		
Multiple-choice questionnaire					✓
Individual task	✓	✓			
Learning log		✓			
Portfolio of work	✓		✓		✓

You might also find it useful to construct a similar grid but this time with task set against the type of person undertaking the assessment. This grid might start off looking like this:

Task/Mode	tutor assessed	self-assessed	peer assessed	employer assessed	tutor moderated
Individual task		✓			✓
Essay			✓		
Seen examination	✓				
Group project			✓	✓	
Multiple-choice questionnaire		✓			
Individual task			✓		✓
Learning log		✓	✓		✓
Portfolio of work	✓		✓	✓	

Look across both grids and in particular at the ways that the ticks are distributed. Ask yourself the following two questions:

- Are you satisfied with the way in which the ticks are distributed over both grids or is there a tendency for ticks to be concentrated in certain areas of either grid?
- In your view are there some valid methods of assessing students, eg, self-assessment, peer assessment, group presentations, learning logs, which do not appear to receive due emphasis, or are absent, from the assessment programme?

If you are not satisfied with the assessment programme, consider how you and your colleagues might address this issue.

What data would you need to collect to be in a position to convince course managers that, for example, unseen examinations or assessor/assessed examinations, both of which are described below, are worthy additions to the range and variety of methods that are used to assess students?

Use the information you have collected as the basis for a departmental paper which puts forward a rational argument for a revised assessment programme.

Examinations

In attempting to answer the questions in the research task above, you might wish to consider, for example, unseen timed examinations and whether or not this form of assessment constitutes a valid method of measuring student learning as defined by the various aims and objectives of the course under scrutiny. You could find out if the amount of time students spend revising for examinations is time well spent; does it lead to effective long-term learning? Many students joke about learning things for examinations only to forget everything as soon as they have left the examination room. If this characterization has any element of truth in it, then it does raise important issues which you might like to consider further; for example:

- What are unseen examinations for?
- What do they really test?
- What is the extent of the match between the functions of examinations and the complete set of course aims and objectives?

In the typical examination scenario many students attempt desperately to second-guess what was in the examiner's mind when he or she set the paper. In some circumstances, of course, the person who set the questions may not be the person who taught that part of the course being examined – a situation which makes it very difficult for students to predict what is about to come up in an examination and therefore to focus their revision. The seen examination is one way to address the issue of focusing students' minds towards a more effective use of the time available for revision. Even so, you may still wish to ask the three questions above.

An approach to examinations which is even more novel than seen examinations, and at the moment is adopted by a relatively few institutions, in effect rolls-up into one person the functions of examination question provider (lecturer) and supplier of examination answers (student). In this approach, students, having studied a particular course, are then required to supply, as part of their assessment, a number of questions appropriate to that course together with a model answer for each of the questions they have set. The assessment then comprises consideration of the quality of both the answers and the questions. (A point to bear in mind here is that students sometimes answer a question badly, not because of any lack of ability or effort but because of an absence of clarity on the part of the person who wrote the question.) It might be argued that requiring students to write examination questions and then answer them is only an (enlightened) extension of the seen examination in which students are normally given the paper around two weeks prior to answering the questions which they do under normal examination conditions. You might like to explore the quality of student experience and learning resulting from the various kinds of examination mentioned above.

Mapping Assessment Criteria to Course Aims and Objectives

In this section we discuss the extent to which course aims and objectives, as mediated through the approaches to teaching and learning adopted by a course teaching team, become embodied within the criteria used to assess students. Since overall aims and objectives should guide approaches to teaching and learning, which in turn might be expected to inform assessment practice, it goes without saying that one would expect to find a high level of match between course aims and objectives and the criteria used to assess students. To us this last point, in theory at least, is uncontentious, and therefore the objective of this section is to enable you to investigate the extent to which this match is evident in practice.

RESEARCH TASK. ANALYSING THE MATCH BETWEEN DESIRED LEARNING OUTCOMES AND ASSESSMENT CRITERIA

Undertake an audit of one of the course components that you teach on. If possible, select a component your institution has written and developed in its entirety rather than one developed from a syllabus that has been set by an external body.

Compile a list of the stated student outcomes for this component:

- aims;
- objectives;
- learning outcomes;
- competences.

(For a comprehensive list of all these outcomes, you may need to refer to the original course validation documents.)

Collect a copy of all the assignments, including required coursework, used to assess students studying this component; also collect copies of any assignment guidelines given to students.

Focus on the assessment criteria themselves. Match the student outcomes of the component with the criteria that are used to assess students. (To determine the complete list of assessment criteria you may find it necessary to look at the assessment criteria for the whole course as well as the criteria provided on individual assignment sheets.) You may find it useful to construct a grid as in the previous research task with, this time, stated student outcomes along one axis, and assessment criteria along the other. To help you undertake this task, but more importantly to analyse the results, you may find it helpful to answer the following questions: answers to each one of them could act as a spur to action – perhaps some form of curriculum development coupled with a piece of evaluative research.

- Is the match between the aims and objectives of the course and the criteria used to assess students acceptable?
- Within the formal assessment process, are some aims and objectives overly assessed while others receive little or no attention?
- Are some assessment criteria expressed in ways which do not map onto the aims and objectives of your component?
- Are there some criteria which although not expressed explicitly in component aims and objectives are nevertheless used to assess students? Do these implicit assessment criteria form part of the stated aims and objectives of the course as a whole?

From your analysis of the match between the stated learning outcomes of the component and the assessment criteria, identify action for change that you could recommend to course managers.

Use your results as the basis for a publication, either in the form of a short departmental discussion document or a more extensive paper for submission to one of the journals listed at the back of this book. If you are new to research and research writing, the in-house paper and the ensuing discussion and feedback might give you the confidence and incentive to redraft your paper so as to make it suitable for an external audience; experienced researchers may want to opt for a journal article straight away.

Did you find it a simple matter to undertake the mapping exercise in the research task above, or were some assessment criteria expressed in ways which made it difficult to map them onto the stated learning outcomes? For the purposes of the discussion which follows we shall assume that you were able to complete the task, even if it was with some 'creative judgements'. If it was not possible to undertake this mapping, then you may need to consider whether important issues with respect to quality control and quality assessment need to be resolved by component/course managers: you may also need to consider whether it is necessary to rewrite or revise the assessment criteria and/or the learning outcomes so as to ensure a closer match between them.

The previous research task should have revealed the extent to which the criteria used to assess students map onto the aims and objectives of the component under consideration. One purpose of this analysis was to enable you to identify which aspects of your assessment practice, if any, need to be reviewed in more depth. The focus of the tasks outlined in this chapter so far has been assessment and course aims, but equally the focus could have been the match between styles of teaching and course aims, or the match between teaching and assessment.

Implicit Criteria

An issue which may have surfaced during the previous research task, and which warrants specific mention here, concerns whether or not there are some criteria that are used to assess students but which are not featured explicitly either in course aims and objectives or in assessment or competence criteria. Whether or not these unstated criteria have any significant impact on the assessment outcomes of individual students may well be reflected by what is termed the 'content validity' of the assessment tasks – the extent to which the tasks, when taken together, constitute a valid measure of what they are (explicitly) supposed to measure.

Associated with any assessment task there are likely to be some 'enabling' qualities which, without a satisfactory level of prior understanding or competence, prevent students from undertaking that task in a way that enables them to demonstrate their true capabilities with respect to the assessment criteria. These enabling qualities may well be ones which students should have acquired previously, either because they have completed satisfactorily an earlier component of the course, or because they constitute a course entry requirement.

The enabling quality that comes to mind most readily, but which often is not to be found within the formally stated assessment criteria, is the ability of students to express in writing their ideas, knowledge and understanding. You could investigate here how often you or your colleagues penalize students for poor English, such as spelling, grammar, syntax, and so on. In making this point we are not suggesting that it is wrong to penalize students in this way, but simply to indicate that enhancing students' abilities to express themselves in correct English might be an important objective, and therefore assessment criterion, for many courses in further and higher education. You might like to consider including this criterion explicitly within your course(s).

Students whose command of English is poor, including those students who do not have English as their first language, may well be penalized unfairly. The forms of assessment that you use – perhaps an overemphasis on written tasks – may not enable them to demonstrate fully what they know, understand and can do. In situations such as these students may be penalized doubly: first, because of their poor writing skills and second, because they are not able to express themselves in ways that communicate to you, the assessor, their full understanding of the material being assessed.

The issue of penalizing students whose oral and written language skills are poor may be clearer for students whose first language is English but less clear for others. Consider, for example, the action of the European Union, and hence the UK government, in encouraging and enabling student mobility within the Union: you might like to look at your institution's policy regarding language and assessment in respect of students it has recruited from abroad, for example the EU and the Asia-Pacific Region. To help resolve this issue you might decide to go back and consider more fundamental questions, such as the purpose of a particular assignment.

The extent to which students should be penalized for their poor use of English is a very contentious issue and most certainly it is one which you and your colleagues could investigate further within your own department or institution. At least two significant questions emerge. First, the one discussed already: is your institution penalizing unfairly students whose command of English, for whatever reason, is poor? Second, if one major aim of the assessment process is to enable students to demonstrate fully what they know, understand and can do, is the assessment programme for your component or course when considered as a whole fit for its purpose? Are some of your students not able to demonstrate the full range of their capabilities simply because the assessment programme, with its overemphasis on written assignments, does not enable them to do this?

RESEARCH TASK. ANALYSING INTENDED AND UNINTENDED ASSESSMENT DEMANDS ON STUDENTS

Choose a component you teach on; this need not be one from the course chosen in the first research task in this chapter but if possible choose a component for which you have some direct responsibility for the assignments that are set.

Obtain a copy of all formally and informally assessed required assignments for this component.

Analyse each assignment in turn to assess the sorts of the demands being placed on students. Don't base your analysis on the assessment criteria – that was the focus for the previous research task; instead undertake your analysis from the actual assignments themselves. Ask:

- Are the demands solely course-specific, requiring students to deploy skills, knowledge, understanding, etc which they have acquired at some earlier stage in the course/component, or are some demands more general in nature?
- What level of demand is placed on students' general skills? (For example, consider and evaluate the reading demands imposed by questions.)
- How many words do students have to read before they can understand fully what is required of them?
- Are the questions ambiguous or expressed in ways which make comprehension difficult?
- Do questions contain non-technical language which is difficult for students to comprehend?

Having analysed the formal and informal assignments for this component, what changes might you make so as to reduce the unintended demands on students, for example, those associated with 'language'? If the reading demand is high, how can this be reduced or simplified?

For more reliable answers to some of these questions you may find it

---

helpful to obtain evidence directly from students; for example, you could take note of the clarification questions they ask when you give out an assignment. Equally, you could also undertake an analysis of how students answered – perhaps incorrectly – the assignment when you come to assess it.

Use the results of your analysis as the basis for a departmental paper which evaluates the level of language and allied skills required by the assessment programme for the component under scrutiny.

Having completed your analysis of the language demands of assignments you might still feel that for a particular assignment a written answer is the only way to assess the knowledge and understanding you are trying to assess. However, before you decide finally, why not ask some students for their views on this matter?

For a more comprehensive review of the language demands you could look at assignments set by other colleagues who teach on the same course(s) as you. (Don't forget to ask them for their permission to use their assignments in this way.) Having completed this task you might like to set the demands which you make in the wider context by looking at other courses in your institution, even similar courses in other institutions.

Non-traditional Forms of Assessment

If you are worried about the unnecessary language demands associated with a particular piece of assessed work then you might like to consider alternative ways, other than a free written response, to assess the knowledge and understanding that you are trying to focus on. For example, you could try:

- setting a practical task instead of, or in addition to, a written one;
- using a series of structured questions, each one requiring a short written answer;
- using a multiple-choice format;
- getting students, either individually or in small groups, to make a presentation to the remainder of their class, or other appropriate audience, and then to answer questions from the audience;
- interviewing students, either individually or in small groups.

When considering student presentations for assessment purposes and, in particular, the quality of the audience participation, you may wish to explore the effect of the assessor's presence in the audience. You could look at what happens when you ask probing questions of:

- the group as a whole;
- individual members of the presentation team, especially if you think that one or two members of the group have not pulled their weight (a frequent complaint of aggrieved students). For a discussion of issues relating to how the total mark awarded to a group is distributed to students so as to reflect individual student contribution to the group effort, and how you might research these issues, see Conway *et al.* (1993).

The interview, sometimes called the *viva*, although a very effective means of drawing out students' knowledge and understanding, is a very time-consuming method of assessment and as such should be used sparingly. You could investigate the one-to-one interview as a viable method of assessment when compared with, for example, group forms of assessment.

Who Does the Assessing?

So far we have looked at the 'what' of assessment, the nature and types of tasks that are used to assess students. We turn now to a discussion of the second important aspect of methods of assessment, namely 'who' does the assessment. In this context we are referring to the person who actually makes the assessment, and not to the person who is responsible for the academic rigour and quality of the assessments that are made.

In the past, who has made the assessments and who has had first-line responsibility for the rigour and quality of those assessments has tended to be the same person – you, the lecturer. However, recent trends in further and higher education have called into question whether it is feasible, let alone desirable, for this situation to continue. We have discussed already some of the major consequences for academic staff of the expansion in numbers of students in further and higher education. Three significant consequences of this expansion have some bearing on the discussion in this section: changes to staff student ratios (SSRs); changes to the level of funding and the impact that this has had on the ways students are expected to learn; and the increase in the range and diversity of courses provided by any one institution. The main points to recognize here are:

- an increase in the average size of student groups means that it is no longer realistic to expect tutors to be able to assess work to the same level of detail as in times gone by. To illustrate this point, about ten years ago SSRs in UK higher education institutions were in the region of 10:1, today they are nearer 25:1;
- tutors may be having to teach more hours overall, but fewer hours to any one group of students. This means that any given tutor will teach an increased number of students because the number of groups taught and the number of students per group have both increased. The probable outcome is that unless changes occur to the ways in which students are assessed, over the course of a single academic year, the number of assignments each tutor is required to assess is likely to increase significantly;
- tutors may have to undertake tasks which are additional to their normal, but increased, teaching load; undertaking research/scholarly activity and producing publications of a quality that enables them to be submitted to research assessment exercise panels, and undertaking administrative tasks in respect of funding agency returns are examples of just two such activities.

These changes present an intractable situation for most institutions. At the same time as individual tutors are being required to take on increased work loads, institutions are being required to demonstrate that quality has not only been maintained but that it has been enhanced. The situation can be exacerbated by the fact that the increase in the demand for a tutor's time is likely to be far greater than can ever be met simply by individual tutors working that much harder and longer.

We have, quite deliberately, presented the negative side of the situation: for institutions, reducing the amount of time a tutor spends assessing an individual student saves money and with the unit of resource – the amount of money an institution receives for each funded student on a course – being driven down, that is very good news. The issue of adopting methods of assessment which save on tutor time need not be only a matter of financial accounting.

- You may wish to explore whether or not the move towards less traditional methods of assessing students can be justified on educational grounds as well.
- You could investigate if savings in tutor time with respect to assessment can be achieved without any diminution in quality. (For a discussion of peer and self-assessment and how well these approaches correlate with assessments undertaken by tutors, see

Oldfield and Macalpine, 1995.)
- You might identify the ways in which your institution is managing this situation, and then explore what impacts these management decisions are having, or are likely to have, on quality.

RESEARCH TASK. ANALYSING COSTS AND BENEFITS OF NON-TRADITIONAL FORMS OF ASSESSMENT

Return to the first research task in this chapter and to the different ways in which your students are assessed. Make a list of the ways of assessing students which contribute, or could contribute if the assignment were suitably modified, to a saving in the amount of time individual tutors spend on assessment.
Sort these methods into general categories, for instance:

- requiring students to produce a group, rather than an individual, report of a project;
- requiring students to give presentations which can be assessed on the spot;
- asking students to assess one another's work (peer assessment);
- asking students to assess their own work (self-assessment);
- asking someone else to assess the work, for example, a teaching assistant, a research student, an employer who is involved with the workplace learning element of the course;
- moderating other people's assessments by second marking only a sample of assignments.

Construct a questionnaire or an interview schedule to help you find answers to the following questions (more details on how to construct a questionnaire or to write an interview schedule can be found in Chapter 7):

- What are the educational benefits of these new methods of assessment?
- What is the extent to which these benefits are borne out in practice?
- What do students see as the benefits of making presentations to their peers or to local employers?
- What do students gain from assessing their own or their peers' work?
- What do course managers see as the benefits of these 'new' approaches to assessment?
- What do employers see as the benefits?

In order to answer the questions above you may also need to consider:

- how you will collect the data and who you will talk to;
- what data you will collect and how you will record and analyse them.

Again, refer to Chapter 7 to find out more details of how you might do this.

Now consider the disadvantages – for students, lecturers, course managers, employers – of using these new methods of assessment.

Consult relevant journals (see the list of journals at the back of this book) to find out how other tutors have addressed the issue of the reduced amount of time available for assessment.

Use the results of your research as the basis for an institutional paper or a journal article which reviews this whole area and which discusses the costs and benefits of these 'new' approaches to assessment.

As a result of your work, are there any new assessment techniques which you recommend be introduced into your department? Monitor their implementation and then evaluate their level of success.

Looking at the responses from the various people you have questioned during the last research task, were you surprised, even disappointed, with the opinions you received? For example, did institutional managers and students offer differing perspectives on the situation? With moves towards so-called performance indicators as measures of quality, there is the danger that, for purposes of comparison, institutions are being required by central government and/or funding agencies to make important what is measurable and reliable at the expense of what is valid (and therefore important) but unreliable. In this respect institutions are being encouraged (required?) to report simple, readily available quantifiable data as outcome measures of quality (Morrison *et al.*, 1995). The point to remember here, of course, is that a move such as this will change what is seen as important in the process of educating students and, as a consequence, is likely to distort the educational experiences they receive.

Annotated Reading List

Bennett, Y (1993) 'The validity and reliability of assessments and self-assessments of work-based learning', *Assessment and Evaluation in Higher Education*, 18, 2, 83–94.
As its title suggests, this paper explores different meanings of the concepts 'reliability' and 'validity' as they relate to the assessment of work-based experiences. The paper also provides a very useful source of definitions of both concepts and as such makes a valuable complement to the book by Frith and Macintosh.
Cashian, P (1995) 'The assessment of BTEC common skills in higher education: a review of one course team's experience', *Journal of Further and Higher Education*, 19, 1, 19–29.

Apart from providing some useful starting points for a consideration of skills-based assessment, this paper provides a good model of a journal article that you might wish to write.

References

Conway, R, Kember, D, Sivan, A and Wu, M (1993) 'Peer assessment of an individual's contribution to a group project', *Assessment and Evaluation in Higher Education*, 18, 1, 45–56.

Frith, D and Macintosh, H (1984) *A Teacher's Guide to Assessment*, Cheltenham: Stanley Thornes.

Morrison, H, Magennis, S and Carey, L (1995) 'Performance indicators and league tables: a call for standards', *Higher Education Quarterly*, 49, 2, 128–45.

Oldfield, K and Macalpine, J (1995) 'Peer and self-assessment at tertiary level: an experiential report', *Assessment and Evaluation in Higher Education*, 20, 1, 125–32.

Qualter, A (1988) 'Serving many purposes. Aggregating scores – does it work?', *Curriculum*, 9, 3, 159–64.

Chapter 5

Managing Assessment

In this chapter, we explore the issue of time as it relates to assessment, especially as it impinges upon students and lecturers. We look at assessment as a complex, human interactive process that arouses strong feelings and requires the development of management skills and strategies. We suggest ways of looking at issues of efficiency and effectiveness as they apply to assessment, and in particular as they relate to the values held by some of the stakeholders in the educational process. We explore attempts to link teacher performance and assessment and discuss ways that student performance can be monitored and recorded.

Time Issues in Assessment

The pace of change in colleges and universities has perhaps been greatest in the area of assessment. The management of this change has to take into account the development of new forms of assessment, often underpinned by a view of teaching and learning that is at variance with that traditionally valued in some colleges and universities. Halsey (1992) found that low morale, disappointment and resentment towards this development have built up among UK lecturers in recent years. You could investigate the extent to which low morale is caused by feelings of overwork, deskilling and changes in the role of the college and university. Typically, new forms of assessment require lecturers to acquire new skills and attitudes. This can be a painful process that makes different, and sometimes uncomfortable, demands on staff and students. Staff and student skill development becomes a management issue that is worth some investigation. Equally, the perceptions and feelings of those involved in the new forms of assessment, the administrators (managers and course leaders), those that have to implement them (the lecturers and students) and the consumers (employers and members of the community), are important issues that should be acknowledged when new forms of assessment are introduced.

New forms of assessment and increases in 'productivity' (especially in terms of larger student groups) have created time dilemmas for lecturers. In order to cope with the new assessment burdens, lecturers may need to adopt a variety of strategies. These strategies can make an interesting starting point for investigation.

RESEARCH TASK. CONDUCTING A SURVEY INTO LECTURERS' ASSESSMENT ACTIVITY

Conduct a survey to discover the range of assessment-related activities that lecturers undertake; for example:

- setting examination papers;
- conducting individual tutorials related to assessment;
- marking essays.

Use the results to determine headings for a simple pro forma to discover how much time lecturers spend on assessment-related activity in a given time period (a week, a term, a semester or a year); for example:

Please estimate in minutes how much time you spent on the following assessment-related tasks in the past week.* Please include preparation time, informal assessment (for instance, diagnostic marking of students' work), administration and providing feedback as well as formal assessment.

	Preparation	Assessing	Giving feedback	Administration
Setting exam papers				
Conducting tutorials				
Marking				
Moderation meetings etc.				

(See Chapter 7 of this book or Ashcroft et al., 1996, for details of how to construct a questionnaire.) Discuss the results of this survey and your interpretation of them with an experienced colleague.

Use the results of the survey as a starting point for an investigation into lecturers' use of time as regards the range and type of assessment tasks that they are involved with.

*If you use a week as your time period, you may wish to repeat your survey several times to discover typical assessment loads across the year.

Perhaps the greatest tension in assessment for lecturers is that between the maintenance of quality and standards in giving feedback to students and the need to cope with greater student numbers. We have already pointed out in Chapter 4 that this tension implies that lecturers should find ways of doing things which are more time-effective. The alternatives are to do the same things but to a lower standard, or for lecturers to work longer hours. Neither of these seems to be wise or sustainable in the longer term. You might investigate whether, nevertheless, time dilemmas lead lecturers into using these unproductive strategies rather than looking for new ways of assessing students.

Heywood (1989) suggests that the most satisfactory method for capturing the complex outcomes of higher-level courses is the use of a multiple strategy approach to assessment. If this is true, the pressure to consider new ways of assessing students may be beneficial to educational quality (see Chapter 7). Moore and Davidson (1994) suggest that lecturers should consider radical alternatives to the traditional forms of assessment. They point out that many of these alternatives have significant benefits for student learning. For instance, the ability to work as part of a team and to communicate with a variety of audiences is valued in the workplace.

Students may be assessed as part of a team, according to their performance or the way they explore a controversy. A group product, such as a report, a display, a student-led seminar or a video can then be assessed using less tutor-time than might be needed to mark several individual assignments. Each of the students may be awarded the same marks or the group may be awarded a pool of marks and allowed to decide whether to award them equally or according to the contributions of each of the participants. You might investigate whether such tasks encourage students to develop particular management skills, to take responsibility for each other, to bear the consequences of irresponsibility or to develop particular communication skills. You could look at the process of group discussion – arguing about alternatives, listening to each other's perspectives on the issues, and whether these processes deepen student understanding of the issues and their ability to analyse them. Goldfinch (1994) suggests various ways of checking the tendency of some students to give over-generous marks. If you have access to relevant data, you could explore the effectiveness of these techniques.

Students may be encouraged to mark their own work or that of others. This should reduce the time that the lecturer must spend marking. You might get students to double and triple mark assignments and to discuss their feedback and written comments. You could moderate the process and spot mark some assignments to assess the extent to which students are using comparable standards. Alternatively, you may wish to explore the effects of various techniques to ensure their comparability: for instance, giving students clear guidelines as to what should be expected within an answer, and criteria by which they might assess the quality of the feedback that they give to their peers. You may be interested in the effects on their learning from the process of peer marking compared with that resulting from the original assignment.

You may be worried that student marking may be unreliable and that they may not be able to provide the quality of feedback that you could. You may wish to investigate whether, given the right conditions and good guidelines, student comments are as useful to the recipient as your own. You could also measure the time students give each assignment that they are marking, compared with that provided by a tutor. You might also look at whether the process of double or triple marking and the student discussion of the process improve student markers' and/or markees' knowledge or study skills.

RESEARCH TASK. EXPLORING PEER ASSESSMENT AND FEEDBACK

Use student markers, organized into triads, according to the following process:

- Students complete the assignment.
- You provide detailed guidance, including the assessment criteria and the characteristics of an excellent, very good, good, adequate, poor and very poor answer.
- Each student marks the assignment of one of his or her peers and drafts written feedback on the assignment.
- Each student's assignment is double and triple marked (blind) by two other students.
- The second and third markers draft their own comments on the work.
- The marks and draft comments are discussed within each triad of markers.
- Each triad of markers agrees a mark and final version of the comments.
- These, together with the assignment, are given back to the student concerned.

During this process you should be available as a resource to the student group.

Find a colleague within your subject who is willing to cooperate with you in an investigation into student marking of a course assignment.

- You mark a similar assignment in the traditional way.
- Ask your colleague to double mark (blind) the sets of assignments first marked by you and by the students and write their own comments for each.
- Compare the marks and comments provided by the lecturer and students with your own. Note the differences and similarities.

Ask various lecturers and students what they consider to be the feature of good feedback on assignments to students, for example:

use of praise;
precise indicators of areas of strength;
precise indicators as to how the assignment might be improved.

Analyse your comments, those of the lecturer and those of the students, using categories revealed by your survey.

Use the results of this exercise as a starting point for an investigation into the reliability of student versus lecturer marking (perhaps at different levels or in various contexts), or into the quality of written feedback provided by students rather than lecturers.

You might test the validity of your results and the interpretation of them by using various research methods (eg, questionnaire and interview) and by discussing your interpretation of the results with both lecturers and students. (See Chapter 7 for more details of how to do this.)

There are time issues for students in coping with the assessment schemes that they experience. These can have interesting ramifications: you may wish to explore the students' use of time as it relates to assessment in some of the same ways suggested above for lecturers.

Students may experience difficulties with scheduling their work. Modular courses can create particular problems in the timing of students' workloads. Assignment deadlines may bunch, and there may be little opportunity for lecturers to take into account how their combined demands impact on particular students. The Council for National Academic Awards (1989) points out that in modular schemes, each module is usually assessed on completion. This assessment is important to the student, since it makes a measured contribution to their award, but it can lead to a proliferation of assessments, and this creates a burden for students. In addition, students may experience a lack of balance between different forms of assessment and suffer a lack of progression in the expectations made on them. External examiners and moderators may be used to safeguard students from inappropriate demands, but they may also fail to get an overview of individual student experience. These issues could make an interesting focus for research.

RESEARCH TASK. MATCHING COURSE MODE AND STUDENT PROGRESS

Interrogate your institution's database to find out the drop-out and failure rates on different types of course (modular, linear, open learning, etc), within either the full-time or part-time category. (See Ashcroft *et al.*, 1996, for a discussion of issues in database interrogation.)

Where you find contrasting patterns of course completion between different types of provision, conduct a series of interviews with students, ex-students and lecturers to discover the extent to which these differences may be related to assessment and, where there are differences, what seem to be the variables.

Use your results as the starting point for a discussion of assessment patterns as an influence on completion rates of students on particular types or levels of course. (Be careful not to make too many claims for your data, as there will be many confounding variables.)

People Issues in Assessment

Changes in assessment are likely to incur human costs – emotional as well as financial. It is easy to ignore people's feelings when implementing change and to imagine that change can be a purely rational process. Bryman *et al.* (1994) are among those who demonstrate that such an approach within the complex, interactive context of education may result in a compliance that is largely procedural and that lacks the necessary commitment to improve standards.

Brown and Knight (1994) discuss the human side of implementing change, specifically in the context of assessment. They argue that lecturers may have to change their ideas of what works: this can be painful. Change is likely to challenge many firmly, if sometimes erroneously, held ideas about assessment. These include the notion that the ability to undertake a statistical analysis of data in some way makes that data more valid and reliable. This relates to the idea that numbers applied to written forms of assessment are inherently more reliable than scores applied to practical, visual or oral work and also that numerical scores are more accurate than verbal or written comment. Perhaps both ideas have their roots in the exaggerated respect that some non-mathematicians have for information expressed as numbers and for the moderation process. Other problems may result from the attachment we tend to have to forms of teaching and learning that we experienced during our own formal education. This may lead to a belief in the 'rightness' of traditional approaches that may underpin the common complaint of each generation that the tests and challenges faced by the younger generation are less rigorous than those that went before.

Brown and Knight (op cit) suggest that these attitudes may go some way to explain why content change in education seems to be more easily achieved than changes in methods of teaching, learning or assessment. Additionally, content change tends to involve a relatively small group of people in curriculum planning. Changes in educational processes, such as assessment, may need to be effected across departments and institutions, if students on interdisciplinary courses are to be ensured breadth and balance in assessment methods, as well as some development in the demands made of them as their programme of study progresses. If such problems can be overcome, much innovation is possible, as lecturers across the institution share practice and support each other's experimentation. You might investigate the benefits (for instance, the development of a common sense of identity) as assessment becomes a matter for cross-institution debate.

Brown and Knight (op cit) point out that such cross-institution development has its own risks. First, within today's 'publish or die' climate, there are real opportunity costs to other models of research in an excessive focus on immediate and regular publication. In addition, the logic of commonality, especially in systems that allow for credit accumulation and transfer between institutions, may lead to the idea that a national system of assessment is desirable. Such a system might represent a threat to academic freedom, and act as a break to real innovation, which may depend on groups of lecturers trying out ideas that are not initially accepted by the majority.

There are problems for lecturers in deciding what should be assessed. These are often human issues that arouse powerful emotions. We have already discussed in Chapter 4 the various forms of assessment that will be typically included within a quality scheme. These would include the assessment of skills, and possibly attitudes, as well as knowledge. Formative as well as summative assessment may be included. The definition of what should be assessed, and what aspects of this assessment should count within the award, are often problematic issues that you may wish to investigate.

RESEARCH TASK. EXPLORING ASSESSMENT IN THE NON-COGNITIVE DOMAIN

Set up a variety of scenarios involving student problems that are not unambiguously within the academic domain. Ask lecturers to comment on the scenarios. For instance, you might set up a scenario as follows:

> You have a group of students who exhibit poor social skills in seminars, tending to dominate discussion and/or trivialize the contribution of others.

- Would you design your programme to develop particular social skills?
- Would you systematically assess the students' development of these skills?
- If so, how would you do so?

(See Ashcroft et al., 1996 for more about scenario analysis.)

Check your interpretation of each point made with the lecturer.

Use the results from this enquiry as the starting point for an investigation into the match between lecturers' goals in fostering students' development in the non-cognitive domain and the assessment methods that they use.

You might check the preliminary results of your investigation by looking at responses from lecturers from various disciplines, teaching on vocational or non-vocational courses or teaching at various levels.

You may wish to investigate the stress caused to staff and students by the introduction of changes in assessment. Evans and Turner (1993) suggest that new initiatives should only be introduced when the time is right. Timeliness is a concept that may be viewed from the point of view of various parties to the education process. For instance, innovation may need to be linked to a vision of the future that is shared by those responsible for its implementation. Changes in the assessment process may be particularly problematic in more traditional institutions, where regulations and ordinances may restrict change. In these circumstances, you might choose to investigate methods to involve and gain the support of key management staff.

Where innovative assessment is a feature of one course or department, rather than part of the institutional culture, students may find changes in assessment especially difficult to cope with. Brown and Knight (op cit) suggest that we should take student views into account. They provide a summary of evidence contained in various case studies to suggest that most students want to be assessed fairly and broadly. You could investigate whether prompt feedback, reference to specific criteria, or the quantity of feedback is most important to students. You may go on to explore the different assessment preferences of students and any link between the variety of assessment methods and the provision of equality of opportunity.

If innovation in assessment is to be successful, those involved in the change (for example, support staff, lecturers, managers, employers and students) will need to be clear about the motivation that underlies the change and the anticipated consequences. This clarity requires much discussion. You might investigate the tension between individual autonomy and systematic change. People's attitudes are unlikely to change positively if they are simply 'told'. The needs of all those involved – employers, support staff, part-time staff, occasional tutors, and students, as well as those of tenured lecturers – are likely to be central to the success of any innovation. In assessing such success, you may need to recognize that, even in ideal circumstances, it may be unreasonable to expect all aspects of an innovation to work, at least in the first instance. Successful change probably depends as much on long-term commitment, flexibility and persistence as it does on initial preparation.

Efficiency and Effectiveness

Questions of efficiency and effectiveness often seem to be in conflict. Society's need for summative assessment may be in conflict with the lecturers' and students' concern with formative assessment as a support for learning. The role of resources within this conflict is an interesting area for investigation.

In the UK, some of the debate about new forms of vocational qualifications such as the NVQ/GNVQ has centred on issues of efficiency and effectiveness. Assessment-led schemes, such as NVQ, are said by some critics to be ineffective. You might explore whether the various participants within such a scheme support this criticism: in particular, whether the scheme is too focused on employability skills and the short-term needs of that industry as it exists at the moment (the ability to 'do the job', at the expense of the knowledge that would enable the student to adapt to new situations). Alternatively, you could look at the criticisms of these schemes on the grounds of efficiency: the time taken by assessment, by moderation and by the detailed and atomized specification of competence. You could explore whether these schemes may have drawn lecturer time away from the development of programmes to foster more general transferable skills and knowledge. Interestingly, following the recent review of the National Curriculum, assessment in schools within England and Wales has moved in the opposite direction. Detailed specification of levels within subjects has been replaced by more general descriptions which state the typical behaviours that indicate whether or not a level of competence and knowledge has been broadly achieved. The extent to which such level descriptors could replace competence statements in post-compulsory education has not yet been explored.

The effectiveness and efficiency of an assessment scheme could be explored from the employer's point of view; for instance:

- how existing skills of employees can be assessed;
- whether this requires costly processes to accredit them;
- the costs and benefits of this processes vis-a-vis a more traditional training programme;
- whether the training framework should be tailored to the needs of the industry in a more precise way (for example, in terms of the timing or form of training); and/or
- whether the employer generally knows exactly what he or she is buying in terms of the minimum levels of competence, when purchasing training or employing a person with a particular qualification.

Education may be seen as preparation for a job or as preparation for a full and satisfying life. The notion that education is of benefit in its own right has declined in recent years. Instead, education's usefulness for the economy has been stressed. This focus has led to the emphasis on assessment of competence over the development of knowledge and understanding for its own sake. One of the problems that may emerge with assessment-led schemes is the encouragement of surface approaches to learning (see Marton and Saljo, 1984, for more details of deep and surface approaches to learning). Ashcroft and Foreman-Peck (1994) have described how certain approaches to assessment may encourage students to take an instrumental approach to learning. You could explore which types of assessment scheme encourage students to focus their time on 'playing the system' in order to get desired results, rather than focusing on the learning itself.

In subjects where reflection is an important objective, schemes that encourage an instrumental approach to learning can be a threat to the effectiveness of a programme. Assessment in these circumstances can become the means of ensuring discipline in the student body. You might explore educational cultures that include the belief that, 'if it is not assessed, the students will not do it', and the effect of such a culture on the volume and type of assessment the students experience. (See Chapter 4 for another perspective on these issues.)

RESEARCH TASK. INVESTIGATING THE WAYS LECTURERS BALANCE ASSESSMENT AND OTHER DEMANDS

Interview several lecturers who are having to teach increasingly large student groups to discover the ways in which they may be managing larger groups of students, for example:

- getting students to monitor their own learning by:

  - self-assessment;
  - marking their own work according to model answers;
  - peer assessment of work (perhaps moderated by the lecturer);
  - determining criteria and marking guidelines.

- reducing the marking volume by:

  - marking only a random sample of the work produced by a student (perhaps with the students peer-marking the rest);
  - getting students to produce more concentrated work (eg, displays, summaries of issues, models and diagrams);
  - using computer-marked tests.

- doing more of the marking in class time by:

  - marking student presentations;
  - using class tests.

Use the results to design a questionnaire that will enable you to start to explore the extent to which lecturers adapt their management of the assessment task to the student numbers they have to deal with. Check out the questions you have selected and your reasons for selecting them with some of the lecturers that you interviewed.

Send the questionnaire to lecturers working in various contexts (eg, in different subject areas and/or in different colleges or universities)

Your analysis of the results could be the basis of a reflective paper, exploring the potential for changes in the management of assessment in certain contexts to cope with an expansion in student numbers.

Opportunity Costs in Managing Assessment

In considering assessment issues, managers have to weigh up the opportunities offered by changing or retaining existing practice, against the costs of doing so. This can be an interesting area of investigation. The establishment of opportunity costs within education is by no means a precise business. For example, there is the problem in establishing who bears the cost and who receives the benefit. This may be quite complex. For instance, formal examinations may not be ideal occasions for fostering learning since they:

- usually focus students on to remembering, and second-guessing, the examination setter's intention;
- encourage surface learning, rather than learning for its own sake;
- create anxiety so that students may not demonstrate their full abilities;
- may favour one group of students who cope well with examinations over other potentially able groups;
- provide minimal opportunity for feedback to students:
- may lead to superficial and inaccurate marking because of a lack of time between sitting the examination and the deadline for the completion of marking;
- enable assessment of only a limited range of possible learning.

Given these 'costs', the significance accorded to examinations by government, some educational institutions and others seems hard to understand. Where resources are limited, some of the educational disadvantages of examinations outlined above may become managerial advantages. For instance, formal examinations tend to limit the amount of words that are written and usually involve tight marking deadlines, so that marking can only be done as thoroughly as time allows. This means that marking may take up less of the academic year and occupy fewer academic weeks than other forms of assessment. Examinations provide a numerical mark that represents a form of normative assessment uncomplicated by qualitative data, giving a simple measure for sorting applicants for employment, further study and so on. You could look at the variety of bureaucratic functions that rely upon such data. In looking at the opportunity costs of formal examinations, you may wish to analyse who bears the costs (in relation to the relative power of the various parties to the examination process) and to whom benefits accrue: students, lecturers, managers of educational institutions, government, or employers.

RESEARCH TASK. USING FOCUS GROUPS TO EXPLORE ASSESSMENT ISSUES

Create the following focus groups (see Ashcroft et al., 1996, or Morgan, 1993, for how focus groups work):

a group of employers;
a group of students;
a group of institutional managers;
a group of lecturers.

Discuss the opportunities and costs of non-traditional forms of assessment by going through the following process:

Provide each group with a list of the types of assessment tasks that might be found in non-traditional forms of assessment.
Ask each person to write an individual list of the benefits and costs of each form of assessment from their particular point of view.
Ask the group to share their views.
Ask the group to create a composite list of costs and benefits.

Use the results from your focus groups to compile a list of statements about the costs and benefits of non-traditional forms of assessment. Use these categories to create a questionnaire which includes a set of statements that reflect the perceived costs and benefits of non-traditional assessment.

Refine the statements and the reasoning that lies behind them by discussing them with members of your original focus groups.

Ask other representatives of the various stakeholders in the educational process whose perceptions you are interested in exploring to complete the questionnaire. Get the respondents to rate their agreement with each of the statements on a 5-point scale, for example, 1: strongly disagree; 2: disagree; 3: neutral; 4: agree; and 5: strongly agree. Again on a 5-point scale, ask them to rate the importance of each issue from their point of view, for example, 1: totally irrelevant; 2: fairly unimportant; 3: neutral; 4: fairly important; and 5: very important.

Discuss the results and your interpretation with members of your original focus groups. Use the survey as the basis of a paper on the opportunities and costs of non-traditional forms of assessment for the various stakeholders in education.

In considering opportunity costs, issues of social justice often intrude. We have suggested that you may wish to investigate whether the relatively powerless may bear the costs of change, or the lack of it, while the powerful reap the benefits. You may also want to explore the long-term effects of such costs on the students concerned. Boud (1994) suggests that students cannot escape the effects of bad assessment, and that poor experiences can have profound adverse effects on learning. He states that there is often a distinction made between the purposes of formative assessment (mainly to aid learning) and those of summative assessment (mainly to measure the outcomes of learning) but that this distinction may be false. Summative assessment should also serve learning. Where it does not, it will have negative effects on the learning it assesses and on future learning. Each assessment gives a coded message about the intention of the examiner, the nature of learning and the nature of the student as a learner. Boud terms this backwash effect on learning of past assessments, 'consequential validity'. Consequential validity is a concept that seems of particular importance to those interested in managing the teaching, learning and assessment process and is worth some investigation.

RESEARCH TASK. EXPLORING STUDENTS' ASSESSMENT HISTORIES

Ask groups of students to write their 'biography' of being assessed over a specified time period (for instance, during their school years). Ask them to include:

– all assessment events that have had an effect on them;
– an account of what that effect was;
– an estimate of the importance that effect has had on their later life and development.

You might ask the students to plot the assessment events as a 'temperature chart', with a time line across the bottom and a line indicating neutrality across the middle, with a positive zone above and a negative zone below, for example:

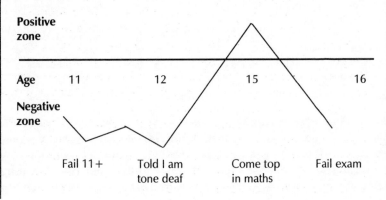

Use the results of the survey as a starting point for an investigation, using 'life stories', into the persistence of the effects of assessment experiences on students' life chances, learning and/or self-concept.

Use interviews and questionnaires to validate the emerging results from this investigation and your interpretation of them.

Use what you have found out for a discursive paper on the effects of assessment experience on students' life chances.

Assessment and Teacher Performance

The new culture of accountability within colleges and universities in the developed world has led funders to seek new ways for measuring the performance of staff, students and institutions. Because assessment often results in a numerical score, it is an attractive 'ready' measure for such accountability purposes. In this section, we describe some of the issues inherent in such measurement that might be worth investigation, before going on to consider more innovative and qualitative measures, especially those relating to student progress and achievement, that may support and enhance learning.

There have been various attempts in recent years to suggest that student achievement can be a measure of teaching effectiveness. This notion underpins the linkage of funding in the UK colleges and universities with student completion and success rates. It also underpins the publication of school and college league tables of results.

The notion of using student achievement as a measure of teaching effectiveness is superficially attractive: after all, it is simple to understand and makes comparisons between individual and department performance easy and apparently objective. Some writers, such as Crooks (1988), assert that while using student assessment may be useful for the purposes of the teacher's individual development as an indicative feature of the effectiveness of their actions, it is inappropriate for the bureaucratic purposes of accountability. You may wish to explore the extent to which the results a teacher, department or institution obtains are dependent on factors that cannot be easily measured, controlled or accounted for, such as the nature of the assessment tasks.

The effect of performance indicators that emphasize 'success' rates is an interesting area. You could try to discover whether they encourage institutions and departments to play safe: to emphasize outcome levels at the expense of a notion of value added, and therefore to deny opportunities to disadvantaged groups. Where funding depends upon results, you could explore the risk of grade inflation. Finally, the variation of marking standards and the type and specificity of criteria in various contexts could make an interesting study: for instance, where the institution sets and marks its own examinations and assignments, and where examining is undertaken by an external organization.

RESEARCH TASK. INVESTIGATING 'GOOD' PRACTICE IN ASSESSMENT

Ask various groups of students to discuss and list good lecturer practice in assessment and to identify indicators of positive lecturer performance in this area, for example:

- provides specific aims for all assessment tasks;
- provides clear criteria for each assessment task;
- provides prompt feedback;
- provides meaningful feedback.

Use the results from this survey as a starting point to investigate student expectations of lecturers in relation to assessment.

You could go on to investigate the differences between student definitions of good practice and lecturer definitions, or the relationship between these definitions and written guidelines supplied by the educational institution or actual lecturer behaviour.

Use your results to write a discursive paper on perceptions of good practice in assessment.

Recording Student Progress and Achievement

In recent years there has been increasing emphasis on continuous methods of recording students' ongoing achievement. These have developed into more sophisticated systems for profiling a range of student achievement. Assister and Shaw (1993) describe records of achievement as a way of saying what we know about students. They suggest that the process of profiling achievement is more important than the finished document itself. This process seems to depend upon a dialogue between student and tutors and involves students in goal setting and the assessment of personal as well as academic development.

Records of achievement may also serve a summative purpose. They may include prescribed outcomes that must be included, as well as other elements where the student may negotiate the way that outcomes may be measured or the type of evidence that may be included. This reflects the dual purpose of some documents: that of a record of actual achievement and also a framework for self-assessment and development. The tension between these dual purposes could make an interesting starting point for investigation. You might explore whether, and if so how, employers and other end-users of the assessment process actually use such documents.

RESEARCH TASK. ANALYSING DOCUMENTATION RELATING TO RECORDING PROGRESS AND ACHIEVEMENT

Find a department in your institution that is introducing records of achievement. Ask if you may analyse planning documents and records to investigate *some* of the following:

- the objectives of the scheme;
- the nature and extent of involvement in the planning by:
  lecturers
  institutional managers
  support staff
  students
  employers
  other end users;
- how the records of achievement are to be integrated into teaching, learning and/or assessment schemes;
- how the record of achievement relates to other curriculum development;
- staff development issues;
- equal opportunity issues;
- quality assurance issues.

Check your preliminary results and your interpretations of them with staff and managers who are involved in the planning.

You could write up your findings as a reflective paper about the ways that various interest groups have influenced the agenda, and/or the emphasis given to various issues within the planning process.

The business of recording and monitoring student performance has become a more prominent issue in recent years. For instance, in the UK, records of progress and achievement have been developed in schools and have been found to enhance children's learning. They are now compulsory for all school leavers. Increasingly, colleges and universities are developing their own systems of recording a fuller picture of student achievement (rather than concentrating solely on that captured by the formal assessment system that leads to an award). These are often used to monitor progress in order to help students to record in full their development of the skills and attitudes appropriate to their level of study. You could investigate the evidence to support the claim that such systematic monitoring of students' progress and the recording of their achievement supports their learning and prevents the wastage of talent when students fail or drop out of courses.

The various systems that have developed do not conform to any single model of assessment. Some rely upon students' self-assessment, supported by regular 'appraisal' interviews with lecturers who help them to set appropriate targets; others rely to a greater extent on the judgements of lecturers and the results of formal assessments. The effects and effectiveness of these two approaches could make an interesting area of investigation.

Some universities in the UK are moving towards more systematic and formal recording of student progress and performance in the shape of credit accumulation and transfer schemes. These are now also being explored within the 16 to 19 age group. Robertson (1993) points out that the framework within the United States is the most well established in the world and may provide a model for other countries. Within the European Union, a pilot has been established arising from the ERAS-MUS student exchange programme within universities. Rainbow (1993) points out that there seems to be a need for a national and international record of progress and achievement that indicates for each certificate or diploma the level of achievement, the grade points accumulated at that level, the composition of the programme of study, and other relevant information. You could explore the extent to which such a scheme can be sufficient to describe a students' standard of achievement, or whether the various parties to the assessment process feel that it should be supplemented by qualitative data about the student's personal, social, academic and other achievements.

Whatever system is adopted, there is a need for agreement on the specification of the aims and anticipated outcomes from the scheme, the degree of specification of the content, of control of the data to be included, and ownership of the record.

The form of any record of achievement can play an important part in the accreditation of prior learning. Institutions are increasingly willing to accept learning from other contexts for the purpose of non-traditional entry to further and higher education, provided that the candidate's achievement is recorded in a form that can be used to establish equivalence to the formally assessed learning that represents the normal entry qualification. If the record demonstrates clear evidence that the candidate has achieved the level and type of learning required within the institution, some may also be willing to admit candidates to courses with advanced standing.

RESEARCH TASK. INVESTIGATING ATTITUDES OF ADMISSIONS TUTORS TO NON-TRADITIONAL APPLICANTS

Talk with course leaders and tutors with responsibility for interviewing and admitting students to various disciplines within your institution about their policies relating to:

- applicants with non-traditional entry profiles;
- applicants requesting admission with advanced standing on to a programme of study;
- students requesting transfer to other courses within or outside the institution.

For example, you could ask:

A potential student without formal qualifications in your subject, but with good relevant work experience, approaches the college/university wanting to do your course. Take me through everything that would typically happen to him or her.
What criteria would you apply in deciding whether or not his or her experience is acceptable for entry?
Under what circumstances would you allow admission with advanced standing onto a course?

Read Wilson's (1993) paper. Use his ideas on the necessary rules within a credit accumulation and transfer scheme relating to accumulation, transfer, and progression as a framework for analysing the responses you collect.
Discuss and refine your analysis with a lecturer who is experienced in the admissions process.
Use your results as a starting point for an enquiry into the formal and informal rules relating to the accreditation of prior learning or credit accumulation and transfer operating within different contexts.

When recording and monitoring progress, it is necessary to decide whether or not to adopt a criterion- or norm-referenced approach to the definition of achievement. Each has advantages and disadvantages that are worth investigating. Norm-referencing involves comparing the performance of a student with that normally expected of other students studying at that level. Criterion-referencing refers to assessing a student's performance against previously specified indicators of successful student action, often expressed as competences.

Criterion-referenced assessment is said to have the advantage of clarity as far as the student is concerned. You could explore whether or not students involved in such schemes actually experience these advantages: for instance, whether they can see more clearly what has to be done in order to achieve a particular criterion and if they know when they have achieved it. You might also explore the effect on motivation of assessment as and when the student is ready, as opposed to waiting until fixed points within the course.

You could also investigate whether problems emerge with criterion-referenced schemes. For instance, the Further Education Unit (1994) points out that such schemes may be criticized for encouraging a behaviourist, reductionist approach that fails to take into account the dynamic nature of much vocational and non-vocational learning. You could look at whether such approaches lead to over-specification and so to atomization of defined outcomes in an attempt to achieve reliability at the expense of validity and efficiency. Criterion-referenced assessment may appear to be more transparent but, in reality, valid assessment may often depend upon contextual judgements and interpretation. You could explore whether, in practice, criterion-referenced assessment emphasizes directly applicable skills at the expense of understandings and knowledge that may be needed in the future.

The basic problem of criterion-referenced assessment is that it is easiest to apply in its pure form to 'can do' situations. As soon as you start to make judgements about 'how well you can do', you are into the sphere of norm-referencing. Such judgements depend upon knowing what you would normally expect from a student at a particular level and stage within a programme. In situations where you are expecting reflection and evidence of understanding, norm-referencing may be more appropriate. You may wish to explore the techniques that various educational institutions use to establish such norm-referencing, and the extent to which these can be said to be sufficiently validated.

Most records of achievement focus on positive aspects of student learning. They describe student success and only by omission do they identify lack of success. Unfortunately, tutors also need to keep good records for other purposes. You may wish to investigate the formal and informal record-keeping systems that lecturers use, and the purposes of each: for instance, systems for managing marginal students' performance, for recording help and guidance and for identifying those who are at risk.

Annotated Reading List

Assister, A and Shaw, E (1993) (eds) *Using Records of Achievement in Higher Education*, London: Kogan Page.
A collection of papers which analyses various issues and describes systems of recording student achievement in use in the UK.

Atkins, M, Beatie, J and Dockrell, WB (1993) *Assessment Issues in Education*, report produced by the School of Education, University of Newcastle.
This is an analysis of the purposes of higher education and their implications for assessment policy at national, institutional and departmental level.

Brown, S and Knight, P (1994) *Assessing Learners in Higher Education*, London: Kogan Page.
A particularly useful book that deals with definitions and principles, methods and organizational issues in assessment.

Gibbs, G (1984 and 1985) *Alternatives in Assessment 1* and *Alternatives in Assessment 2*, London: SEDA.
These are collections of very short case studies of different methods of assessment. Volume 1 looks at self- and peer assessment and 2 at computer-based assessment.

Further Education Unit (1993) *Discussing Credit*, London: FEU.
A collection of occasional papers relating to the FEU's proposal for a national post-16 credit accumulation and transfer framework within the UK.

Marks, S (1993) *Assessment in Technology: Faculty-wide evaluation of assessment methods to improve quality assessment and feedback*, Kingston University (mimeo copies available from Faculty of Technology or Educational Development Unit, Kingston University).
This provides a model of how you might write up a case study describing the introduction of innovative and more efficient forms of assessment

Wolf, A (1993) *Assessment Issues and Problems in a Criterion-based System: FEU Occasional Paper 2*, London: FEU.
A critical evaluation of criterion-referenced assessment that identifies some of the uncertainties in such a system.

References

Ashcroft, K and Foreman-Peck, L (1994) *Managing Teaching and Learning in Further and Higher Education*, London: Falmer Press.

Ashcroft, K, Bigger, S and Coates, D (1996) *Researching into Equal Opportunities in Colleges and Universities*, London: Kogan Page.

Assister, A and Shaw, E (1993) 'Records of achievement: background, definitions and uses', in Assister, A and Shaw, E (eds) *Using Records of Achievement in Higher Education*, London: Kogan Page.

Boud, D (1994) 'Assessment for learning', SEDA National Conference: Assessment for Learning in Higher Education, 16–18 May, Telford.

Brown, S and Knight, P (1994) *Assessing Learners in Higher Education*, London: Kogan Page.

Bryman, A, Haslam, C and Webb, A (1994) 'Performance appraisal in UK universities: a case of procedural compliance', *Assessment and Evaluation in Higher Education*, 19, 3, 175–88.

Council for National Academic Awards (1989) *Going Modular. Information Services Discussion Paper 2*, London: CNAA.

Crooks, T (1988) *Assessing Student Performance: Green Guide Number 8*, Kensington, NSW: HERSA.

Evans, N and Turner, A (1993) *The Potential of the Assessment of Experiential Learning in Universities*, London: Learning for Experience Trust.

Further Education Unit (1994) *Examining Assessment*, London: FEU.

Goldfinch, J (1994) 'Further developments in peer assessment of group projects', *Assessment and Evaluation in Higher Education*, 19, 1, 29–33.

Halsey, A (1992) *Decline of Donnish Dominion: The British academic professions in the twentieth century*, Oxford: Clarendon Press.

Heywood, J (1989) *Assessment in Higher Education*, Chichester: Wiley.

Marton, F and Saljo, R (1984) 'Approaches to learning', in Marton, F, Hounsell, DJ and Entwistle, NJ (eds) *The Experience of Learning*, Edinburgh: Scottish Academic Press.

Morgan, DL (ed.) (1993) *Successful Focus Groups*, London: Sage.

Moore, I and Davidson, S (1994) 'Assessing more students effectively in more time', SEDA National Conference: Assessment for Learning in Higher Education, 16–18 May, Telford.

Rainbow, B (1993) 'Post compulsory education: A national certificate and diploma framework', in FEU, *Discussing Credit*, London: FEU.

Robertson, D (1993) 'Credit frameworks: an international comparison', in FEU, *Discussing Credit*, London: FEU.

Wilson, P (1993) 'Developing a post-16 credit accumulation and transfer framework: the technical specification', in FEU, *Discussing Credit*, London: FEU.

Chapter 6

Models of Evaluation

In this chapter we consider evaluation as a process by which the effectiveness of educational interventions can be assessed. In selecting the model and approach to be used for evaluation, we suggest that various issues should be considered. These include the scale or scope of the evaluation process. You will need to consider whether a smaller amount of relatively simple data from a large sample will serve particular evaluation purposes better than a wide range of more complex data from a smaller sample. The choice that is made will depend in part upon the purposes of the evaluation. We examine summative purposes of evaluation: for instance, to ensure accountability to bodies or individuals remote from the teaching context, where quantitative data within predetermined categories with predetermined criteria for success may be the most appropriate approach. We also look at the formative purposes of evaluation: for instance, the desire to improve your practice, where qualitative data that include unintended as well as intended processes and outcomes may be particularly useful.

Within this analysis, we refer constantly to the various audiences and interest groups involved in the evaluative process. These include the 'consumers' of education: the parents, students and employers of graduating students. These people may have some overlapping expectations and criteria of success, but also many concerns that do not necessarily overlap. The providers of the educational process, teachers and institutional managers, will also each have their own expectations and criteria. Finally, those who fund and seek to control the service will have very particular needs and interests. Each of these stakeholders in education has an interest in particular models of evaluation and forms of data. Each can exercise some power. Although those that control the resources seem to be in the ascendancy at the moment, we suggest that their interests should not be the only ones to be considered.

Evaluation and Reflective Practice

Evaluation is basic to reflective practice. It provides the raw material for reflection, the evidence to underpin changes in action and the means by which open-mindedness and responsibility are exercised. We have conceptualized reflective action in teaching as an evaluation-led activity in which evaluation and the collection of data about the context for action leads to reflection on the significance of that data, and that in turn informs planning, provision and action. On the completion of this cycle, evaluation again takes place, this time into the effectiveness of action, leading to another cycle of reflection, planning and action, as shown in Figure 6.1.

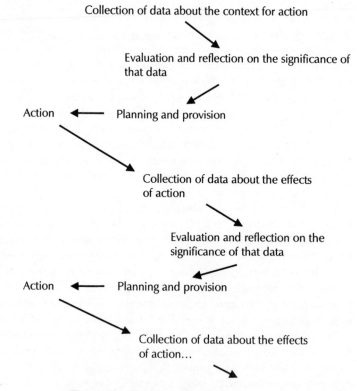

Figure 6.1 *Model of reflective action*

This model of reflection has much in common with the model of action research developed by Stenhouse (1987) and others (for instance, Carr and Kemmis, 1986 and Elliott, 1991). It also relates closely to Argyris and Schon's (1974) notion of the development of theory from practice. Of course, action research tends to be focused on a problem, and reflective practice is not necessarily problem-based (unless the problem is 'How do I become a more effective lecturer?'). On the other hand, both require enquiry into practice, are centred on the improvement of practice, and each may empower the lecturer and are based on the notion that the practitioner is the best person to determine foci for evaluation and to control and interpret the resulting data. The close relationship between the notion of reflective practice and action research makes action research a particularly appropriate model for an evaluation-based enquiry into your practice.

Action research is a good method of improving practice, but it may suffer from the following disadvantages:

- the results may be situation-specific, and may not generalize to other contexts;
- the results are unlikely to be verifiable;
- the researcher is an actor in the situation, and so may be particularly liable to misinterpret what is going on;
- the researcher may be asking the wrong questions;
- the subjects of the research are likely to know the researcher well, and therefore their responses may be influenced by power differentials or other interpersonal factors;
- the researcher may be unaware of the particular ethical issues involved in insider research.

These disadvantages may be minimized if you:

- use more than one method to collect data about the problem and the effects of action (this is known as triangulation);
- discuss your definitions, methods and interpretation of results at all stages with your subjects and with experienced colleagues (this is another form of triangulation);
- are open-minded and willing to change your definition of the problem, your methods and your interpretation of results in the light of your experience and discussion with others;
- recognize that your values are part of the research context and should be made explicit in your reporting;
- are modest about what you claim for your results.

RESEARCH TASK. THE PROCESS OF ACTION RESEARCH

Identify a problem in your teaching that may be common to other lecturers (for example, ensuring that all students in a group receive a fair share of your attention).

Use the action research model to enquire into the context of the problem, to decide on a possible intervention and to investigate the effectiveness of that intervention.

At each stage:

- share your planning and reflection with one or more colleagues; and
- keep detailed notes about what you did, your conversations with colleagues, what happened and your reflections, as they occur.

The process of action research involves undertaking at least two cycles of enquiry as follows (adapted from Kemmis, 1988):

Identify the problem that will be the focus for your enquiry:
    Whose problem is it?
    Why is it important?
Find out as much as you can about the context in which it occurs:
    What is happening now?
    Why is it a problem?
    For whom is it a problem?
    When does it occur and how often?
    What form does it take?
    What triggers it?
    What are the alternative explanations for the problem?

Discuss your interpretation of the problem with colleagues and/or students. Decide on an intervention that might improve the situation:

What might a better situation look like?
Why would it be better?

Plan the intervention in some detail.

What actions might improve the situation?
How should they be sequenced?
What criteria would indicate 'success' in dealing with the situation?

Discuss your plan with colleagues and/or students.
    Implement the plan.
    Collect data on the effect of the intervention on the problem:

What techniques will you use to collect your data?
What are the advantages and disadvantages of each?

How might you triangulate findings (can you seek views from various participants in the process, or use more than one data collection technique)?

Evaluate the data:

Do any key words or phrases reoccur in your written records?
Do your data need re-examining in more detail?
Are your data sufficient to draw conclusions or inferences?

Discuss your evaluation with colleagues and/or students.
    Revise the plan:

Are new ways of looking at the problem emerging from the data?
Does your initial focus or research question need to be reformulated?
What values and assumptions about education were implied by your original approach?
Do these need revising?
What ethical issues are raised by your research?

Discuss your plan with colleagues and/or students.
    Implement the revised plan.
    Repeat the data collection/evaluation cycle.
    Look at Kemmis (1982) and/or Deakin University (1988) for more details of how to go about such a study.
    Write up your research for one of the journals that specialize in action research in education.

Evaluation is a means of exploring a range of foci at a variety of levels. For example, you might look at the effects of action at the level of the individual lesson, a linked range of activities (for instance a particular project), a scheme of work or module, or at the level of a whole programme or course. Alternatively, you might wish to look at particular issues across a range of activities. For instance, you might wish to explore students' study skill acquisition, equal opportunities issues or the quality of your questioning.

You may wish to look in some detail at the perspectives or experience of particular stakeholders in education. For example, you may decide to evaluate the needs, abilities and progress of certain individuals or groups of students (see Chapter 7; Ashcroft and Peacock, 1993, also provide an example of such a study). Alternatively, you might wish to explore learning more directly, perhaps looking at students' learning strategies, perceptions and involvement in their programme of study.

RESEARCH TASK. INVESTIGATING THE LINK BETWEEN TEACHING AND LEARNING

Decide on an aspect of the link between student experience and your teaching that you want to explore: for example, the link between the teaching methods you use and the students' approach to the tasks set in terms of surface and deeper approaches to learning (see Gibbs, 1992, or Marton and Saljo, 1984, for outlines of students' approaches to learning).

Use the questions below based on some of the methods described in the Curriculum in Action project (Open University, 1982) as the basis for your enquiry:

What did the students do?
What did they learn?
How worthwhile was it?
What did I do?
What did I learn?
What am I going to do next?

Discuss your observations and interpretations with colleagues and students.

Use the results of your enquiry as the starting point for a paper that links your experience of reflection in action with the relevant literature.

Students are not the only stakeholders in education whose perspective and experience you might evaluate. Your own experience and behaviour is worth looking at in its own right. You may decide to evaluate teaching issues such as changes in classroom organization or changes in your teaching behaviour or personal issues such as the development of your confidence in teaching or your time management. When you evaluate the effectiveness of your own action, you may need to consider what you really value in education and to what extent these values overlap or conflict with those of others within the system. Some of your criteria for success may be in common with those of others: for instance, establishing a good reputation for the programmes you teach. Others may reflect differences in priorities. For example, institutional managers may be particularly interested in saving money and offering courses as cheaply as is consistent with quality. You may be interested in maximizing the resources devoted to teaching your students.

You may need to consider the morality and educational defensibility of your values in the light of the needs and interests of others. Where evaluation foci are determined solely by the lecturer, there is a danger that the perspectives and interests of other stakeholders in education are ignored. As a reflective practitioner, you may decide that you should make a conscious effort to explore the interests, attitudes, needs and experience of students, employers, funders, managers and the community.

It is also worth exploring the hidden priorities, needs and interests of each of those involved in the educational process. This is an area that is less commonly investigated in the context of colleges and universities, although it has been a focus of research into schooling (see Pollard, 1985, for one approach to such a study). These priorities may include the preservation of self-esteem, the need for social and task satisfaction and the need for order and control.

Evaluation happens within particular educational contexts, but some reports are written as if the variables in education and its context are more or less controllable. In reality, there are many influences upon the success of a programme. Some of these have been identified, together with possible patterns of influences, in the research task below.

RESEARCH TASK. USING EVALUATIVE DIARIES TO EXPLORE STAFF PERSPECTIVES

Ask several colleagues among the support and/or teaching staff at your institution to keep an evaluative diary for a week in which they reflect upon their work: the things that went well, the things that went badly and (most importantly) how they felt about them.

Analyse the resulting diaries to ascertain the categories of factors that often reoccur under the following headings:

- Factors linked to successful action (eg, helpful colleagues);
- Factors linked to unsuccessful action (eg, a lack of resources);
- Feelings linked to successful action (eg, feeling in control);
- Feelings linked to unsuccessful action (eg, frustration).

Discuss your interpretations with the diarists and revise your analysis in the light of these discussions.

What does your analysis imply for the priorities and needs of those who work in educational institutions?

You might link your reflections and analysis to some of the variables influencing educational outcomes outlined in the diagram below.

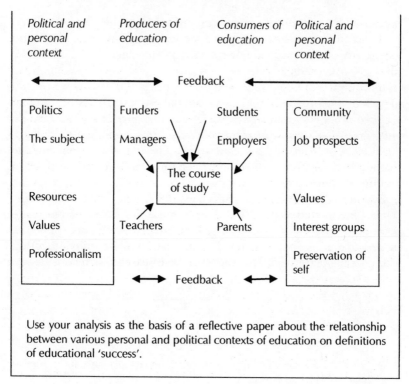

| Political and personal context | Producers of education | Consumers of education | Political and personal context |

Feedback

Politics	Funders	Students	Community
The subject	Managers	Employers	Job prospects
		The course of study	
Resources			Values
Values	Teachers	Parents	Interest groups
Professionalism			Preservation of self

Feedback

Use your analysis as the basis of a reflective paper about the relationship between various personal and political contexts of education on definitions of educational 'success'.

Objective-, Outcome- and Transaction-led Evaluation

Our discussion so far has implied a developmental model of evaluation that is based on the lecturer's (more or less) analytical assessment of those issues that should be the foci for evaluation. There is certainly a place for such evaluation. It may be the main source of genuinely innovative thinking and development. The lecturer's hunch that something should be changed, or could be improved, is often based on a mass of incidental evidence that has come together to form a pattern. Evaluation allows the validity of this evidence and the lecturer's first interpretation to be assessed.

Recently, this kind of semi-intuitive evaluation has been subject to criticism. More structured approaches to evaluation are increasingly seen as more rigorous and therefore more relevant to today's climate of accountability in further and higher education. More structured approaches to evaluation may look at objectives, outcomes or transactions occurring during or resulting from teaching and learning.

In the objectives-led model, the starting point for evaluation is the objectives of the programme of study. The evaluation of objectives depends upon these having been stated in ways that make them observable and/or testable. If you are intending to adopt this model, the demands of evaluation must have been considered at the stage when objectives are formulated. For example, an objective such as, 'To develop students' communication skills' would be insufficiently precise as a basis for evaluation: it would be hard to determine whether students had, or had, not achieved the objective. A more appropriate objective might be, 'To enable students to write accurate laboratory reports that conform to the conventions of the subject'.

The transactional model of evaluation looks at the teaching and learning processes. It enables you to consider issues that are difficult to assess through end-testing, such as the developing quality of the students' relationships with each other. It also allows teaching to be directly observed and assessed. The objective and outcome models of evaluation assume that the quality of teaching can be implied from the student behaviour and learning. This is a problematic association. You may wish to explore the variety of factors that affect student achievement which are independent of the quality of the teaching they receive or the programme they experience.

The outcome-based model of evaluation looks at the achievements of students at the end of a programme of study, and uses these as the basis for an assessment of the quality of that programme. The competence movement in the UK is based on this model. The outcomes of any programme are prespecified in terms of the observable behaviours that would indicate student learning and competence. The content and teaching and learning methods employed are not central to the evaluation process. Similarly, the students' personal development, experience, thinking and attitudes are not of interest in themselves. Success is determined by the presence or absence of certain student behaviours and abilities.

The objective- and outcome-led models of evaluation each focus on student learning. They both assume that this can, and should, be prespecified. They depend upon a definition of evaluation as a process of comparing the actual and anticipated outcomes (or objectives) of education. Unanticipated learning or objectives of students, tutors or others are generally seen as undesirable or to be ignored.

Lloyd-Jones *et al.* (1986) are among the writers who suggest that evaluation should go beyond this to involve judgements about the value and desirability of educational outcomes from the point of view of the various parties to the process. You may decide to adopt a more sophisticated model, based on interaction. You can then analyse the intended objectives, transactions and outcomes of a programme, but also the unintended ones, together with an assessment of whether they are desirable. This model, as described by Tawney (1976) may be conceptualized as shown in Figure 6.2.

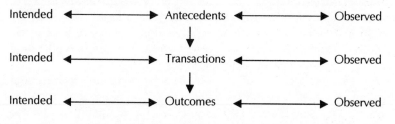

Figure 6.2 *An interactive model of evaluation*

This model allows you to assess unintended antecedents, transactions and outcomes, as well as intended ones. It enables you to consider the context and the 'inputs' into a programme: for instance, the intended level of qualification of students admitted as against those actually enrolled, or the level of resources anticipated as against those actually received. You could use the model to explore the processes of teaching, learning and assessment that were planned and those that occurred, as well as the outcomes of the programme. It may enable you to resolve the dichotomy between 'concurrent' evaluation (evaluation concerned with processes as they happen) and 'subsequent' evaluation (summative evaluation) and to shift the emphasis between them, depending upon the stage of development of a curriculum programme and the intended audience and purpose of the evaluative study.

RESEARCH TASK. USING AN INTERACTIVE MODEL TO
EVALUATE AN EDUCATIONAL INNOVATION

Use Tawney's model as outlined above to evaluate the success of an educational innovation you are involved with (eg, the introduction of a programme based on non-traditional teaching methods).

At all stages, discuss your observations and interpretations with students and colleagues. Document your observations under the categories below:

	Intended features	Observed features
Antecedents		
Student qualifications		
Student prior experience		
Student goals		
Student attitudes		
Sex/age/class ratio of intake		
Management resources available		
Human resources available		
Other resources available		
Other...		
Processes		
Course content		
Course structure		
Course organization		
Course elements (eg, work experience)		
Teaching methods		
Learning behaviour		
Assessment methods		
Evaluation methods		
Student drop-out		
Other...		
Outcomes		
Student skill acquisition		
Student knowledge acquisition		
Student attitude acquisition		
Student assessment results		
Student employment		
Students' further study prospects		
College/departmental reputation		
Other...		

You might use the results of your evaluation as the basis for a paper for one of the journals specializing in small-scale evaluative studies, or you could compare your experience with those of others introducing similar innovations as reported in the research literature.

Purposes of Evaluation: Bureaucratic, Political and Developmental

Evaluation may be demanded and carried out for a variety of purposes. These purposes relate to the interests of the various stakeholders in education. The first set of purposes may be classified as political: evaluation may be used to control the behaviour of individuals, groups or institutions. The motivation is usually to ensure that policy direction is complied with or to satisfy particular interest groups.

Political purposes may embrace the micro-political scene: the institutional or departmental purposes or those of interest groups within the institution or department. You might decide to explore the extent to which managers in various contexts determine the focus of evaluation and thus the developmental direction of teaching teams. For instance, where the increased use of resource-based learning becomes a feature of institutional policy, you might investigate whether it is made a focus of evaluation and, if so, whether teaching teams are encouraged to develop resource-based learning schemes to avoid their non-compliance being exposed within evaluation reports.

Informal grouping within the institution may also exert power and influence through the evaluation system. For instance, a case study approach may enable you to look at change processes within an institution and the role of evaluation within them. You may find that, where a desired change has been blocked by the executive or committee system of the institution, tutors may use the results of evaluation to demonstrate the absolute need for such a change.

The problem with evaluation as a tool for micro-political activity is that the desirable ends of the evaluative enquiry are determined in advance, and therefore evaluation is unlikely to be objective, and may even be dishonest. You may wish to explore whether, where compliance is determined as a criterion for success, institutional policy tends to be seen as a 'good thing' that cannot be questioned and whether evaluation focuses on compliance, at the expense of an examination of the effectiveness of the policy.

Government and other funders of education use evaluation as a major political tool to influence the direction of the education system as a whole. For instance, by determining particular performance indicators as appropriate criteria for success, funders may impose their own interpretation on educational value. Funders may also use evaluation in its wider sense as a means to influence behaviour. They may achieve this by determining that certain aspects of the educational system should be subject to evaluation and providing the funds to enable wide-scale evaluation to take place. In the UK, an example of this is the evaluation of standards in public examinations for the post-16 age group. This ensured that reliability of assessment became a major consideration, rather than, for instance, the validity of assessments (see, for example, Newstead and Dennis, 1994).

Politically driven evaluation at the national or regional level may suffer similar problems to that of micro-political evaluation. The desired outcomes, rather than the desire to discover 'truth', may influence the choice of foci, the funding provided, the criteria for success and the identification of those trusted to undertake the enquiry. It is almost impossible to tell the extent to which political purposes corrupt in a more direct way: for instance, the suppression of the results of an evaluation study that do not support the desired policy direction. The only way that you may be able to investigate this is to undertake confidential case studies of the process of research within politically sensitive projects. If you undertake such a difficult investigation, you need to be aware that the process may be very subtle. For instance, funders may choose evaluators who are broadly sympathetic to the general policy direction that they wish pursued. Alternatively, evaluation questions or the brief may be structured so as to make a particular result more likely.

The second main set of purposes for evaluation are bureaucratic. Administrators in institutions and at government level require evaluative data for a variety of purposes. In the main, they need to compare the performance of one individual, group or institution with that of others, so as to inform funding or distribute other advantages such as promotion. For instance, the Further and Higher Education Funding Councils in the UK are committed to linking funding with teaching quality. Comparative, bureaucratic purposes cannot be met by data that are not standardized. This means that definitions and measures of quality must be determined centrally. Definitions and measures may be most useful if they result in relatively simple numerical data. As a researcher, you may find this institutional data, much of which is published annually, a useful source of information. In interpreting it, you need to be aware of its limitations. Complex qualitative data might provide a more rounded picture of the reality of an institution's teaching and learning quality: in particular, differences in mission, circumstance and intake within various educational contexts.

The final main set of purposes of evaluation is developmental. Developmental evaluation is carried out to improve personal and team effectiveness and professionalism. You might use developmental evaluation to explore similar aspects to those determined by bureaucratic and political purposes, but also more complex and fundamental issues within the process of teaching and learning, such as the approach of lecturers and students to tasks set, their sensitivity, responsibility and personal standards. It can be a particularly appropriate vehicle if you want to get at those aspects that are requisite for reflection. You could use it to explore the interests and needs of a wider set of stakeholders in education than those generally served by political evaluation: students, employers, the community and lecturers, as well as managers and funders.

Some people see the accountability of the teacher as a professional to her or himself and her or his students as the starting point for developmental evaluation. Political and bureaucratic evaluation may sometimes be focused on rooting out incompetence and policing behaviour. Those wishing to use developmental evaluation need to assume that the tutor is competent, well intentioned and interested in improving their teaching and student learning for their own sake, not because otherwise they would be 'exposed', or would lose funding or promotion prospects. In other words, developmental evaluation rests on the notion that teaching is an activity that works best when it relies on the lecturer's own desire to improve their performance for the sake of their students and because of their sense of professionalism.

Because successful development is about self- and team improvement, it takes into account the context for action. It is usually cooperative, rather than competitive. It allows you to explore definitions of 'success' in teaching and learning that rely on a number of factors beyond the lecturer's control: the level of resources, the motivation of students, the support of managers, structures and colleagues and so on. You could use evaluation based on a developmental model to look at how each of these facilitate or obstruct the teaching and learning process.

Developmental evaluation enables you to look forward to see what might be done better, rather than attribute blame for past actions or circumstances. Bureaucratic and political evaluations look backwards, to assess existing performance. They are compatible with, and are sometimes based on, suspicion. Developmental evaluation depends on trust and a belief that, if lecturers and students are to be involved in the evaluation of their own experience and action, they will seek out relevant information and measures and use them in constructive ways to further the interests of the students and other stakeholders in education, rather than use the data to further their own interests. In other words, the assumption is that lecturers are open-minded and responsible enough to own their personal and professional goals and to operate them within the mission of the institution and in the interests of all the stakeholders in education. This is both its strength and its weakness.

Developmental evaluation must be based on honesty. It is not an appropriate model in contexts where there are financial or professional penalties for exposing and exploring problems. Political and bureaucratic evaluation might be more appropriate where poor performance may result in institutional and personal damage, but you need to be aware that those being evaluated may have a vested interest in seeking out and presenting data that will make them look good. To many people, this interest may be inimical to the pursuit of truth that is the basic purpose of research.

Evaluation and the Monitoring Process: Self, Peer, Institutional and Systemic

The evaluation of programmes of study may occur at various levels. Managers, teachers and support staff may be encouraged to take responsibility for seeking, noting, communicating and acting upon the experience and learning of students. This may be achieved in a variety of ways. First, if you believe in a Total Quality Management (TQM) approach (see below for more details about this model), you might try to prime staff and students at all levels to think about how the present ways of doing things could be made better. Of course, you may not be in a position to implement the model fully. Nevertheless, you may be able to operate it in a small way: perhaps by setting up systems to collect information from colleagues and students about a programme you teach or manage. Such systems can be informal: for example, you might regularly review with your students how they are finding their course and what they feel they have learned from it. In addition, more structured systems can be set up, such as suggestion boxes or regular meetings of support or teaching teams.

Evaluation may include some or all of self, peer, institutional or systemic assessment of performance and quality. Self-assessment may include an examination of the values and objectives of either or both of the lecturers and students within a programme and their own assessment (perhaps supported by a lecturer, colleague or manager) of the extent to which their own performance and actions further these values and objectives. The point of self-assessment is the reflection and analysis that the process inspires and the opportunities it offers for identifying clear goals, targets for action, and foci for data collection and further evaluation.

Institutions and departments may also engage in self-assessment. Again the focus tends to be on the mission and objectives identified by the department or institution and performance in the light of these. In the UK today, statements of self-assessment are generally used as a basis of quality assessment by the Higher Education Funding Councils. They can be useful background information if you are interested in researching a range of issues at departmental or institutional level.

Peer assessment can be used at the individual, departmental and institutional levels. Individual lecturers are frequently subject to appraisal. This often involves elements of self-assessment and assessment by a colleague, often a line manager. Peer assessment may involve discussion, consideration of documentation, or the observation of teaching. It may be hard for you to collect evidence about your teaching behaviour without the aid of a colleague to record it, perhaps in note form or on video tape. (See Chapter 7 for more details as to how you might do this.)

RESEARCH TASK. USING PEER REVIEW IN EVALUATION

Find two or more colleagues who are willing to cooperate in a peer review exercise involving observation of their teaching.

Use various published pro formas to assess the quality of each colleague's teaching. (See, for instance, those published by Brown et al., 1993; Gibbs et al., 1988; and Odom-Bradley et al., 1990. See also Bennett et al., 1996 for a fuller discussion of issues involved in structured and unstructured observation of teaching.)

Use each pro forma with each colleague in lessons that include different groups of students and in contrasting contexts (for instance, lecture, seminar and workshop).

Discuss your colleague's interpretation of each lesson, its objectives and the extent to which these were fulfilled. Make your own notes of your impressions of each lesson. Analyse the results from the pro formas.

Use the results of your survey, your reflections and the interviews as the basis of a discursive paper: for example, exploring some of the implications, opportunities and problems in using structured observations of teaching within the appraisal process.

Good practice in evaluation will also include regular, formal monitoring of the components that go to make up a programme of study. This will usually occur at departmental level and may include reports of evaluation meetings of teaching and support teams as well as anonymous feedback from students. The Higher Education Quality Council (1994) suggests that departments should determine performance indicators for courses and progress towards these should be written up within an annual course report. You may wish to investigate whether this is an effective method for identifying problem areas and successes, and for checking on whether appropriate action has been taken.

There is also a place for a periodic review of programmes of study, perhaps every five years, conducted or monitored at institutional level. Such a review can ascertain the extent to which the aims and objectives of a programme remain appropriate, the extent to which the programme continues to meet them and whether, or in what areas, major strategic development of the programme is desirable. Reports of such periodic reviews often contain data that you may find useful as background information for a range of research purposes.

Institutions are responsible for monitoring aspects of the quality of the work that occurs within them. Funding bodies may require assurance that regular evaluation is carried out. For instance, in the UK, the Higher Education Quality Council (1994) recommends that evaluation takes place covering student entry processes and the quality of student experience, including staffing and staff development, support services, student outcomes and standards (see below).

In addition, such internal institutional monitoring may be supplemented by system-wide inspection and review. Inspectors from independent agencies or from other institutions may visit colleges and universities to ascertain the quality of their work. The data from such evaluations can be used to inform research into individual institutions and to shed light on the performance of the further and higher education system as a whole.

Evaluation and Models of Quality

There are a variety of schemes, derived from industry, that have been applied in educational settings, which aim to evaluate and support claims by organizations for quality. Some of these assert that quality may be pursued by the creation of particular systems: for example the Charter Mark and the Investors in People awards (see Freeman, 1993;

Further Education Unit, 1991). Others seek to outline 'universal' principles of good management: for instance TQM and fitness for purpose (see Barnett, 1992; Harvey and Green, 1993). These models are outlined briefly below. A short description of each may be found in Ashcroft and Foreman-Peck (1995).

Investors in People

Investors in People is a UK-based scheme that rests on the assumption that staff are an organization's prime asset. Evaluation is a central feature of this model. First, evaluation of the organization's needs and interests is the basis of the staff development investment made by the organization. Second, the model requires that the effectiveness of that investment should be rigorously assessed. It could be interesting to explore the motivation of colleges and universities in joining such schemes: for instance, to find out whether they see them as providing an independent, evaluative judgement of the quality of their management in relation to staff development or whether they see them in terms of a marketing tool.

The scheme aims to help employers improve performance by linking the setting, communication and evaluation of business goals with staff development. You could explore the extent to which, within educational contexts, the focus is on the institutional mission, rather than national or personal benefit, and whether 'success' is evaluated in these terms. The benchmark against which success is evaluated is adherence to the National Standard for Effective Investment in People. The local Training and Enterprise Council has the responsibility for determining whether a college or university has the evaluative and staff development systems in place to be recognized as an Investor in People. The processes by which these Councils arrive at their assessments could make an interesting study.

Charter Mark Awards

Increasing numbers of colleges and universities in Europe are pursuing accreditation under national standards (for example BS 5750 or ISO 9000). These are measures of institutional systems that were originally applied to the products of commerce and industry. The systems set targets against which each organizational process (for instance, communication) can be evaluated. They do not imply that the products (for instance, the course or programme) are of a high quality, but rather that processes are standardized within them and these processes reach standards set by the institution.

In UK education institutions, Charter Mark awards focus almost exclusively on the quality assurance and student support systems. The institution sets targets and ensures that they are monitored and documented for the whole or part of a system: the award of a Charter Mark does not guarantee that all parts of a student's educational experience will be monitored. Even where the whole of an institution's quality assurance system is covered, the standards set are determined by the institution. The institution or department will be measured against the capability of its systems to monitor whether the standards it sets itself are met, not whether those standards are appropriate. These standards do not have to be high, merely to be achieved. You may wish to explore what types of targets are commonly set by educational institutions, within what areas, and how these targets relate to the priorities of lecturers and students.

RESEARCH TASK. INVESTIGATING INDUSTRIAL MODELS OF QUALITY

Design a questionnaire to find out the attitudes and experience of people involved in Charter Mark and/or Investors in People schemes. Use open-ended questions, such as:

How do you perceive the scheme is operated in your institution?
What is your involvement with the scheme?
What advantages does the scheme have from your point of view?
What disadvantages does the scheme have from your point of view?
What advantages do you believe the scheme has from the students' point of view?
What disadvantages do you believe the scheme has from the students' point of view?

Send the questionnaire to a small sample of students, teachers, support staff and managers working within a college or university that has been involved in such a scheme.

Analyse the results of these questionnaires to find categories of experience that might be included in a questionnaire based on a Likert scale, for example:

Please indicate the strength of your agreement or disagreement with each of the following statements by ticking the relevant box:

	Strongly disagree	Disagree	Neutral	Agree	Strongly agree
The scheme has diverted resources from the support of student learning					
My job satisfaction has increased since the scheme was introduced. etc...					

Check your new questionnaire with an experienced colleague to make sure that it is clear and simple to fill in (see Chapter 7 concerning the possible impact on the analysis of data arising from non-return of questionnaires).

Use the revised questionnaire as the starting point for a paper exploring the experience and attitudes of people involved in a Charter Mark and/or Investors in People scheme.

Total Quality Management

TQM is a model designed to change the culture of the workplace so as to create a constant search for improvement in practices and systems, particularly inputs, processes and outputs. Individual staff effort is supported by extensive training to raise awareness of the guiding principles of TQM and to increase motivation to follow those principles. The principles of TQM rely heavily on ongoing evaluation and include a focus on the 'consumer'. If you are interested in this model, you could seek evidence about student and employer perspectives and experience within and relating to the institution, in order to inform action. TQM also involves management by data. Much of the management data will be evaluative, both quantitative and qualitative. Another principle of TQM is people-based management. This implies that if you are a manager, you must also become an evaluator in order to find ways of investigating the effects of your action upon those you work with. TQM also involves continuous quality improvement. This principle has an obvious relationship with the developmental purposes of evaluation. It implies that you would investigate a range of processes, inputs and outcomes, to see how they might be improved. These come together in the final principle: the creation of an institutional climate that fosters quality at all levels. This relies on the actions and attitudes of senior management, and is therefore less open to direct investigation by lecturers.

Fitness for Purpose

Another model by which quality in education might be assessed is based on the notion of fitness for purpose. This implies that each activity within the institution expresses its purposes in terms of carefully defined aims and outcomes against which performance may be evaluated, and also that each process should be assessed as fit (or not) for its purpose. This model, unlike those outlined above, does not necessarily assume that institutional purposes are paramount, but leaves open the question of whose purposes are to be pursued.

It could be interesting to investigate the strengths and weaknesses of these models in practice. For instance, you might find that, because these models are derived from industry, they neglect a moral dimension. Education is a moral enterprise, and so the needs and interests of the institution cannot be paramount in the same way as those of a business. You could investigate whether each model can cope with success as a problematic notion that includes competing definitions. Reflective practice requires that you look at the long- as well as the short-term consequences of action. You may find that a focus on systems (such as in the Investors in People and Charter Mark schemes) will not achieve this. You could explore the extent to which models such as TQM and 'fitness for purpose' spur staff to seek out, and take into account, the viewpoints of other stakeholders within the educational system.

Annotated Reading List

Arnold, R and Carter, D (1990) *The Use of Performance Indicators*, Slough: EMIE.
An examination of a variety of approaches to performance indicators. Rather school-centred, but the ideas and arguments can be adapted.

Brown, S, Jones, G and Rawnsley, S (1993) *Observing Teaching: SCED Paper 79*, Birmingham: Standing Conference on Educational Development.
This short book contains a number of pro formas and ideas for evaluating teaching through observation.

Burgess, R (1993) *Educational Research and Evaluation for Policy and Practice*, London: Falmer Press.
This book explores the debates in the field of research and evaluation, in particular the problems inherent in evaluation processes. It includes case studies of ways these have been tackled in various contexts.

Deakin University (1988) *The Action Research Reader*, Waun Ponds, Victoria: Deakin University Press.

A set of very useful papers giving a range of theoretical perspectives on the process of action research and describing some projects in action.

Kemmis, S (1982) *The Action Research Planner*, 2nd edn, Waun Ponds, Victoria: Deakin University Press.

A short, simple book that is a useful and practical guide to the process of action research.

Silver, H (1992) *Student Feedback: Issues and Experience.* Council for National Academic Awards Project Report 39, London: CNAA.

A short report that deals with the main issues in seeking student feedback for a variety of purposes.

Tessmer, M (1993) *Planning and Conducting Formative Evaluations: Improving the quality of education and training*, London: Kogan Page.

A critical analysis of formative evaluation and an exploration of techniques.

References

Argyris, C and Schon, D (1974) *Theory into Practice: Increasing professional effectiveness*, London: Jossey-Bass.

Ashcroft, K and Foreman-Peck, L (1995) *The Lecturer's Guide to Quality and Standards in Colleges and Universities*, London: Falmer Press.

Ashcroft, K and Peacock, E (1993) 'An evaluation of the progress, experience and employability of mature students on the BEd course at Westminster College, Oxford', *Assessment and Evaluation in Higher Education*, 18, 1, 57–70.

Barnett, R (1992) *Improving Higher Education: Total quality*, Buckingham: Society for Research into Higher Education/Open University Press.

Bennett, C, Higgins, C and Foreman-Peck, L (1996) *Researching into Teaching Methods in Colleges and Universities*, London: Kogan Page.

Brown, S, Jones, G and Rawnsley, S (1993) *Observing Teaching: SCED Paper 79*, Birmingham: Standing Council on Educational Development.

Carr, W and Kemmis, S (1986) *Becoming Critical: Education, knowledge and action research*, London: Falmer Press.

Deakin University (1988) *The Action Research Reader*, Waun Ponds, Victoria: Deakin University Press.

Elliott, J (1991) *Action Research for Educational Change*, Buckingham: Open University Press.

Freeman, R (1993) *Quality Assurance in Training: How to apply for BS 5750 (ISO 9000) standards*, London: Kegan Paul.

Further Education Unit (1991) *Quality Matters: Business and industry quality models and further education*, London: FEU.

Gibbs, G (1992) *Improving the Quality of Student Learning*, Bristol: Technical and Educational Services.

Gibbs, G, Habeshaw, S and Habeshaw, T (1988) *53 Interesting Ways to Appraise Your Teaching*, Bristol: Technical and Educational Services.

Harvey, L and Green, D (1993) 'Defining quality', *Assessment and Evaluation in Higher Education*, 18, 1, 9–34.

Higher Education Quality Council (1994) *Guidelines on Quality Assurance*, London: HEQC.

Kemmis, S (1982) *The Action Research Planner*, 2nd edn, Waun Ponds, Victoria: Deakin University Press.

Kemmis, S (1988) 'Action research', in Keeves, JP (ed.) *Educational Research, Methodology and Measurement: An international handbook*, Oxford: Pergamon.

Lloyd-Jones, R, Bray, E, Johnston, G, and Curries, R (1986) *Assessment: From principles to action*, London: Macmillan.

Marton, F and Saljo, R (1984) 'Approaches to learning', in Marton, F, Hounsell, DJ and Entwistle, NJ (eds) *The Experience of Learning*, Edinburgh: Scottish Academic Press.

Newstead, S and Dennis, I (1994) 'The reliability of exam marking in psychology: examiners examined', *The Psychologist*, May, 216–19.

Odom-Bradley, M, Howard, S and Larson, JL (1990) *An Advocacy Approach to the Observation and Evaluation of Teachers*, Manhattan, KS: The Master Teacher.

Open University (1982) *Curriculum in Action: Practical classroom evaluation*, Milton Keynes: Open University.

Pollard, A (1985) *The Social World of the Primary School*, London: Holt, Rinehart and Winston.

Stenhouse, L (1987) 'The conduct, analysis and reporting of case study in educational research and evaluation', in Murphy, R and Torrance, H (eds) *Evaluating Education: Issues and methods*, London: Harper and Row.

Tawney, D (1976) *Curriculum Evaluation Today: Trends and implications*, London: Macmillan/Schools Council.

Chapter 7

Methods of Evaluation

With the moves, outlined in Chapter 2, towards greater public account-ability of further and higher education institutions for the money they spend, the collection of data for purposes of institutional evaluation is a relatively new and significant growth area within the post-compulsory educational scene in many countries, the UK included. However, in this chapter we will not focus on this area but instead we will explore more traditional aspects of evaluation; for example, methods of data collec-tion which should help you know more about the teaching and learning processes which take place in your classroom, and how effective these processes are in promoting student learning. We shall discuss in detail only those forms of evaluation which are either tutor/lecturer or insti-tution initiated; only passing reference will be made to those forms of evaluation which are derived from sources external to your institution.

The main aim of this chapter therefore is to provide you with the knowledge, skills and sources of information necessary to enable you to undertake meaningful evaluations of your own professional practice and which also may be undertaken with the minimum of resources, human as well as financial.

The discussion and research activities in this chapter centre around three main themes: *Why evaluate? Who evaluates?* and *How to evaluate.* For example, we shall discuss the benefits of evaluating your own profes-sional practice and the techniques that you might use to gather the information necessary to undertake this evaluation. We shall describe four data-gathering techniques; questionnaires, interviews, analysis of documents, and first-hand observation.

The approach to evaluation which we adopt is not a 'deficit' one, that is of undertaking evaluation in order to remedy some aspect of your work that is wrong or unsatisfactory. Instead we adopt a positive and supportive stance, one which attempts to enable you, as a professional, to maximize opportunities through a recognition that the relationship between teaching and learning (lecturer and students) is an evolving one and as such is subject to continuous change.

Why Evaluate?

Lecturers continuously evaluate their teaching and so for most people the evaluative process is not new; evaluation is part and parcel of most lecturers' day-to-day ongoing teaching. However, one style of teaching where evaluation of this nature does not appear to constitute a significant contribution to the way a session unfolds, and which appears to be on the increase, is the set-piece formal mass lecture. Here the situation only permits the lecturer to make minimum use of any feedback being provided by the student audience; in fact the situation may be such as to lead students into feeling that feedback is not encouraged. However, in small class teaching situations evaluation is ongoing, informal, short-term, and of relevance to the immediate situation. The lecturer receives feedback from students about the learning situation (for example, whether students understand what is being taught) interprets and evaluates this feedback using her or his professional experience and knowledge, and then acts as seems most appropriate. Continuously, almost on a second-by-second basis, lecturers evaluate the effectiveness of their teaching by taking note of, and responding to, the non-verbal behaviour of students (whether or not they are listening to, and engaging with, what the lecturer is saying and doing, whether or not they appear to be interested in what the lecturer is trying to teach them), and by asking students questions and acting upon the answers they give. In fact, to be denied this form of feedback makes teaching an extremely difficult activity to undertake successfully: without feedback the lecturer does not know how best to proceed next. This may be one reason why some lecturers find the mass lecture a somewhat artificial and unrewarding activity, and why some students find it a fairly inefficient way to learn.

The type of evaluation described so far provides you with information which, although collected by informal and unsystematic means, does, nevertheless, enable you to make progress through the session in a way that has most meaning for students. The iterative model of teaching and learning which implicitly emerges from this style of evaluation was introduced in Chapter 6 and relates closely to the model of reflective practice we have already outlined. It may be described as follows:

- plan session;
- begin to teach session – put initial plan into action;
- receive ongoing feedback;
- use feedback to evaluate the effectiveness of the teaching so far;
- teach the next step in the process, having mentally modified your original plan so as to take into account the feedback provided.

How to proceed with the next small step in a learning sequence is only one reason why you need to evaluate your teaching. You may also need to consider the much larger steps: from one session to the next, or from one section of the course to the next. You may need to be more systematic than in the previous approach to evaluation and, perhaps, more objective in the ways that you collect feedback information. You may even need to collect different types of information, such as that provided by short class tests and other forms of student-assessed work.

Taking account of this more formal feedback requires a slight elaboration to the model of teaching and learning described previously:

- plan session(s);
- teach session(s);
- assess and use feedback to evaluate effectiveness of teaching;
- plan next session(s) in the sequence.

Evaluation can be a means of helping to shape your day-to-day, and short- to medium-term, teaching – what might be termed 'formative evaluation'. It is one very important reason for undertaking the kinds of activity mentioned so far in this chapter: it enables you to see where students have got to in the learning process and what you need to provide for next so that they may eventually achieve the longer-term learning aims and objectives that you have set for them. However, this is not the only reason why it is important to engage in the process of evaluation.

At significant points in a course, for example when a particular course component ends, or possibly at the end of a term, a semester or a year, you may find it useful to discuss with your 'clients' (see Chapter 2 to refresh your memory) their perceptions of what you have been teaching and the effectiveness of the methods you have been using to aid students' understanding of course content and processes. Quite a lot of the discussion in Chapter 4 focused on non-traditional approaches to assessment, for example, peer and self-assessment. You might, therefore, wish to research your students' attitudes to these approaches; if you do, compare your results with those of Williams (1992). Depending on the type of course or component being evaluated it may be appropriate to widen the range of people you ask and to include those beyond the boundaries of your classroom, even your institution; for example, in the case of vocational orientated courses you might canvass the views of employers.

Who Evaluates?

Once you undertake evaluations which extend beyond the boundaries of your classroom, the purposes for the evaluation become connected, much more explicitly than in the situations mentioned earlier, with who undertakes the evaluation. For example, informing a lecturer of the effectiveness of their minute-by-minute teaching is probably best undertaken by students in the classes concerned. However, these students are unlikely to be the best people to evaluate how well the course has met the needs of the workplace – employers and ex-student employees may be better equipped to take part in this type of evaluation. The processes and procedures that you might need to take note of when undertaking this type of evaluation are illustrated later on in this chapter by the research task which completes the section on open and closed questions. You might like to investigate how wide your institution casts the net in its attempt to gather comprehensive 'client' opinion and how effective the process is in feeding back to course teams the opinions expressed by 'clients'.

All forms of evaluation can make you feel fairly insecure, even threatened, particularly if you are relatively new to lecturing, or if you have been teaching part of a course which is new or unfamiliar to you. In effect, you are submitting what you consider to be your best attempts to the scrutiny of others. There is nothing new in this since, as mentioned above, your students will be evaluating your work all the time. Nevertheless, you may find it threatening to invite these people to tell you, to your face, their perceptions and opinions. What can be even more threatening is if these views are used for purposes which extend beyond your classroom, even beyond your department or institution, and therefore beyond your control. You may wish to investigate whether or not students also perceive this activity as threatening. They may see you as being in a position to exert influence over their futures, for example whether they pass or fail your component, and may therefore be reticent, or unwilling, to make highly critical but, to them, truthful comments about your component. You may also wish to investigate whether any unintended bias has crept into your institution's methods of evaluation. For example, evaluation questionnaires often ask students to identify points of strength and weakness in their course; an individual student may be perfectly satisfied but, because you have asked for points of weakness, feels compelled to give you some. In other words, an expressed dissatisfaction may not be an expressed complaint. We will follow up some of these points later on in this chapter; the reason for mentioning summative evaluation in detail here is not to discuss student evaluation but to flag the potential that this type of summative evaluation has in respect of curriculum development and, especially, that which relates to major reviews of courses.

Evaluation and Curriculum Development

One point to bear in mind when reviewing the need for curriculum development is that evaluations undertaken by more than one person or group of people can often convey mixed messages. For example, what one group of students in a class liked, another group from the same class did not; what this year's students saw as inappropriate, last year's group saw as appropriate; while employers saw the course as being very appropriate to their needs, students did not. Therefore, before you embark on any significant piece of curriculum development that has been initiated because of evaluative feedback from students or employers you will need to be certain that the necessity for change has been expressed strongly and *consistently*. Where you appear to be getting a clear message, but you are not sure, when you teach that component again, why not focus the evaluation on the issues which have emerged?

Evaluation can provide an objective means of identifying those aspects of a course which could profitably benefit from change. Equally, evaluation can provide you with objective evidence concerning the relevance and effectiveness of the changes that you have put into place. In this way we have identified an extension to the evaluation process described earlier in this chapter, namely:

- teach the component;
- undertake summative evaluation;
- identify specific needs for curriculum change/development;
- modify the curriculum so as to meet identified needs;
- teach the modified component;
- undertake *focused* summative evaluation.

In working through the curriculum development cycle, from identifying needs to meeting them, the model of evaluation which we have developed here moves from an evaluative instrument to one which is focused more tightly around the curriculum development that has taken place. A lecturer who has completed such a process has in fact completed a piece of curriculum development using an approach known as 'action research'. Further discussion of this approach may be found in Chapter

6 and in Bennett *et al.* (1996); for diagrams which illustrate the cycle of action and evaluation/reflection see Hopkins (1993).

RESEARCH TASK. EVALUATION AS A BASIS FOR RESEARCH OR CURRICULUM ENQUIRY

Use evaluation of your teaching as a basis for a piece of research or curriculum enquiry. Use the model outlined above to generate a description of what you have done, from identification of needs through to an evaluation of the effectiveness of the curriculum change. Use this description as the starting point for an article for one of the journals cited at the end of this book.

In your article you would need to describe:

● the context around which the piece of action research took place, including reference to relevant literature;
● the reasons why you undertook an evaluation of the course or component;
● your evaluation instruments, including any trialling and subsequent revisions which took place – these are discussed later on in this chapter;
● how the research was conducted and the data collected;
● the methods by which the data were interpreted – again, more details will be found later on in this chapter;
● the curriculum change(s) that you decided to introduce;
● the focused evaluation instrument;
● your conclusions concerning the effectiveness of the curriculum innovation introduced;
● a bibliography of the work of other authors cited in your article.

So far we have looked at evaluation as a process which is internal to your department or institution, even though some of the people involved, for example ex-students, may be considered to be outside your institution. External processes, often undertaken because of the need to be accountable for how public money is used, also exist. In the UK, organizations such as the Further and Higher Education Funding Councils, OFSTED, the validating body for the courses which you work on (if you teach in the university sector this body is likely to be internal to your institution), all require institutions to have their work evaluated for reasons of public accountability. If you work outside the UK, then which external organizations does your institution have to work with for reasons of public accountability?

We will say little more here about external forms of evaluation except to mention that organizations such as Funding Councils and OFSTED are increasingly using evidence obtained from institutional self-evaluation as a means of contextualizing evidence collected via their own externally devised instruments of evaluation. You might like to compare the validity of these externally devised evaluation instruments with your own, or your institution's, methods of evaluation. (See Chapter 6 for a more detailed discussion of systems of evaluation external to your institution.)

Evaluation Instruments

There is a wide variety of data collection instruments to choose from when you are deciding how to evaluate your work with students; in this section we will consider four main ones: questionnaires, interviews, analysis of relevant documents – in particular student diaries – and direct observation of the teaching–learning situation. The first two instruments are particularly useful for obtaining summative information, that is for evaluating learning outcomes, although they can be used to look at learning inputs and the actual processes associated with teaching and learning. The other two instruments, and in particular direct observation, are useful for evaluating the effectiveness of the learning inputs and the processes normally associated with learning. Both questionnaires and interviews often rely quite heavily on respondent memory as the main means through which data are provided; document analysis and, in particular, direct observation do not. A more detailed comparison of the advantages and disadvantages of different data gathering techniques can be found in Hopkins (1993), and in Cohen and Manion (1994). One issue which you will need to address when undertaking evaluations where the focus is on research, rather than on institutional self-monitoring, is time: Bennett *et al.* (1995) describe how the use of a computer program to aid student evaluation of lectures may contribute to an overall saving in lecturer time.

Questionnaires

The technique that is likely to be used most frequently in further and higher education for the collection of evaluation data is the questionnaire, self-completed by, for example students, tutors and employers. Questionnaires are particularly useful when 'surface' information is required from a large number of people, such as every student on a particular course. Often this type of information is required in summary quantitative form so that it can be included in component and course reports, for example the percentage of students expressing satisfaction with the course organization. Questionnaires have the potential to gather a large amount of data quite quickly. What is more, although this technique works best when the questionnaire is personally administered by the lecturer concerned, questionnaires can be sent through the post and so can be used to canvass the opinion of people (ex-students and employers) who live at some distance. However, it is important to bear in mind that postal questionnaires generally have higher non-response rates than questionnaires administered in person (see below for a discussion of some possible consequences) although inclusion of a stamped addressed envelope can help to reduce the magnitude of this problem. If a questionnaire is going to be used as the main instrument for a piece of research, and especially if it will lead to a publication, it is important that due time and consideration are given over to the questionnaire's construction. Here we wish to raise just a few issues for you to consider; further points to bear in mind when constructing questionnaires are spelled out in Ashcroft *et al.* (1996) and in Bell (1993).

Decide on what data you wish to collect and how you are going to analyse them. If the objective is to collect numerical data then it might be better for you to focus on questions which have either yes/no answers or on questions which are set in a multiple-choice format, including those which require a Likert-style response (see below for more details of Likert-type questions). If you want to collect data which are qualitative then it might be better to focus on questions which are open in format.

You will need to take steps to ensure that the questions are not ambiguous; not everyone interprets written material in the same way that you do, hence the need to trial your questionnaire (see below).

You will also need to ensure that questions or statements, and especially those that require yes/no answers, are simple in structure and are free from conditional clauses. Where questions are complex, break them down into a series of simpler questions; for example, don't use a 'question' such as:

> In Year 2, the introduction of new forms of assessment, such as self-assessment and group assessment of project work, has been very successful and so this year's course has had more relevance than last year's.

Instead ask questions such as:

In Year 2, has the introduction of group assessment of project work been successful? What are the reasons for your response?

You will need to check, through trialling, that none of your questions is leading respondents to a particular answer or point of view, or that the answer to one question is not contained within a previous question. Distracters in multiple-choice questions can often provide answers to subsequent questions and, therefore, you may find it better to locate open-ended (free-response) questions at the beginning of a question-naire and closed (multiple-choice) questions at the end.

You will need to ask yourself and others whether or not your ques-tionnaire encompasses fully the area (domain) you are inquiring into – this is often referred to as the 'content validity'. For example, in a questionnaire about student satisfaction with their course, you will need to ensure that the questions encompass all aspects of the course and not just some of them. A common omission here is to consider only taught elements of the course, such as lectures, and to ignore other aspects of learning, such as assignments and access to resources in the library.

When you are fairly sure that you have got every thing right and in place, pilot your questionnaire by asking a few people, who otherwise would have been part of your sample, to answer the questionnaire and to discuss with you any problems that they had with it.

When you have analysed your data and produced some conclusions ask a few colleagues, preferably those experienced in this type of research, whether, given the data, the conclusions you have come to are valid. This process of asking someone else to check the validity of your interpretations and conclusions is sometimes called 'researcher trian-gulation'.

Generally, quantitative data are simple to collect and straightforward to analyse, especially if all that you require are simple frequency counts and means (averages). Qualitative (non-numerical) data often yield richer conclusions but need more care over their analysis. You may find that you need to ask a colleague with research experience how they would go about, for example, identifying the categories that emerge from your data. Alternatively, you might like to consult one of the many books which deal with the analysis of qualitative data in education settings, such as Maykut and Morehouse (1994).

When undertaking an analysis of data obtained through question-naires, you should pay particular attention to non-response and its possible effects on the validity of any conclusions that you might come to. Everyone who completes one of your questionnaires is likely to be a volunteer, even if, at the time, they do not believe this themselves.

Therefore, you are unlikely to obtain a 100 per cent response rate. As mentioned earlier, administering the questionnaires in person has a positive effect on response rates and therefore you should adopt this approach whenever possible. Non-response would have minimal effect on your data analysis and conclusions were the drop-out to come from people distributed randomly over the spectrum of opinion; unfortunately there is evidence to suggest that this is often not the case. For example, students who are satisfied with their course are less likely to respond to a questionnaire than those who are not. To put this point in an everyday context, people who are pleased with something they have just bought seldom write letters of praise to manufacturers or suppliers; in general, they are more likely to write or 'phone when what they have just bought does not work to their satisfaction. Thus, your questionnaire data may be biased, with a skew towards the dissatisfied end of the spectrum of opinion: you will need to bear in mind this point when evaluating any conclusions you reach.

Individual and Group Interviews

In some respects the interview as a data gathering technique is very similar to a spoken version of the questionnaire; in others it is very different.

Interviews provide the opportunity to pick up non-verbal clues from respondents – *what* they are saying may be considered in the light of *how* they are conveying it, and against body language. What a student says may be taken to indicate a favourable response whereas non-verbally (for example, moving away from you as they speak) they may be communicating a very different opinion.

The interview has the advantage that, provided a rigid (what is called a 'structured') approach is not adopted, the interviewer can add to the list of questions to be asked, and so probe deeply each respondent's answers. However, this flexibility requires that the interviewer guards against asking leading questions, and of dominating the interview. One of the qualities necessary of a successful interviewer is being a good listener.

In terms of the type of data to be collected, interviews are most suited for qualitative data and you may find them most effective when open format questions are asked – the relative merits of closed and open questions are discussed later in this chapter.

Using interviews as a data collection technique has two important drawbacks especially for the part-time researcher who is working with only minimal resources. First, conducting interviews is a very time-consuming, and often tiring, technique. Unlike questionnaires which can be completed by large numbers of people at the same time, interviews can only be carried out effectively with one person or a small number of people at any given time. If you are thinking of using the group interview approach then we suggest that your group size does not exceed six people.

Second, unlike questionnaires where the data are ready for collation as soon as they are completed, interviews present you with a number of significant difficulties. For example, before you start your first interview you will need to have decided how you are going to record your data. You could decide to write down as much as you can of what interviewees say, in which case the interview conversation may not flow smoothly but may need to stop and start to allow you to catch up. Trying to write down more or less verbatim what is said suffers from a further drawback in that you may find yourself concentrating on *remembering* what is said, so that you can write it down accurately, and not on *understanding* what is being said and using this understanding as a basis for the next question. You may also miss meanings that are conveyed through non-verbal language.

As an alternative to writing down what is said, you could tape-record each interview (research ethics demand that you obtain each interviewee's prior permission to do this). Although this approach is likely to overcome many of the difficulties mentioned earlier, tape recording each interview may simply replace these difficulties with new ones. After each interview the data remain hidden – you will have to play back the tape in real time on every occasion that you want to access the data. Even so, comparing what has been said across interviews remains a difficult feat of memory: your only real alternative is to transcribe each interview. However, be wary of doing this since it is likely to take a relatively experienced researcher-cum-typist about four hours to transcribe an interview lasting around 30 minutes. Perhaps you can see now that, although interviewing is a very good data collection technique, it is also very demanding in terms of time and possibly cost, especially if you have to pay someone else to produce the transcriptions for you.

In addition, while questionnaires can, in principle at least, be distributed to everyone, there is little likelihood that you will be able to interview every member of your target group. You will need to develop selection criteria to enable you to identify an interview sample which is representative of the population from which it is drawn. Obviously, the reason for doing this is to try to ensure that the data you collect, and the conclusions you come to, are as similar as possible to those were the whole population to have been interviewed. For a more detailed discussion of how to set up and administer interviews, see Cohen and Manion (1994) and Anderson (1990).

The final point you need to bear in mind when using interviews to collect evaluative data about your teaching is that unlike questionnaires it is often not possible for the interviewee to remain anonymous; interviewees may feel compelled for a variety of reasons to tell you things which either they feel you want to hear or will not jeopardize them in any way. For this reason, asking students to evaluate your teaching through a single group questionnaire may well elicit responses which are substantially different from those were the very same students to be interviewed on a one-to-one basis. Because anonymity during the interview cannot be provided there is a real risk that bias will creep into the data. Furthermore, unlike the bias associated with questionnaires, this bias is likely to skew any conclusions towards the favourable end of the spectrum of opinion.

In terms of the design of a piece of research, particularly where this is concerned with gaining the perceptions of people outside your institution, such as employers and ex-students, a useful strategy to adopt is to use the interview technique as a means of identifying the areas and the issues that need to be explored more fully, and then to use questionnaires as a means of canvassing the opinions of a much larger number of people. You will still need to pilot your questionnaire (for reasons given earlier) but at least you will know where the focus for your study lies, and you will also have a good knowledge of appropriate distracters for any multiple choice questions that you may wish to use – see below for more details.

Using Interviews to Collect Data

In the research task below we describe in broad outline a possible pathway to follow should you decide to use interviews as a basis for collecting evaluative data; it has been adapted from one proposed by Maykut and Morehouse (1994).

RESEARCH TASK. USING INTERVIEWS IN EVALUATION

Identify the purpose and focus for your interview study. Is the purpose to collect evaluative data which will inform next year's teaching of a particular component, or is it to provide summative data for inclusion in an annual course report? Will the focus be on general aspects of the course, such as overall satisfaction with learning outcomes, or will it be more focused, such as the effectiveness of using peer group teaching as an aid to learning?

Having identified the purpose for the study, now decide what broad areas you wish to explore. You may wish to do this through a technique which involves brainstorming linked to concept mapping (Maykut and Morehouse, 1994) provide details of how you might do this).

Decide who, in broad outline, you will interview. Will interviewees be from a single interest group, such as present students, past students, employers, fellow lectures; or will they, collectively, represent more than one interest group, such as students *and* employers?

Analyse your brainstorm to determine which ideas can be left out, and which sequence of ideas is likely to make most logical sense to interviewees.

Decide on the format for your interviews. Will they be open, semi-structured or structured? Now prepare a draft of your interview schedule (the complete set of questions written down in the same order as they will be presented to interviewees) in line with the chosen interview format.

Prepare a standard introduction to the interview which you will use with every interviewee. Include:

- an explanation of the purposes for the interview;
- an explanation as to how interviewees have been selected;
- a statement regarding interviewee anonymity and the use to which you intend to put the data;
- if relevant, a request for permission to tape the interview, including an indication of how the tape will be used.

Prepare, in outline, how you intend to end the interview; don't forget to thank each interviewee for their time.

Pilot the interview with a few people selected from your target population. Revise the interview schedule in the light of feedback from the pilot study.

Begin interviewing.

Analyse the data as soon as they become available, making any minor changes to the interview schedule as necessary.

Undertake the final analysis of the complete set of data, using, for example, the constant comparative method (see Maykut and Morehouse, 1994) for more details on how to do this).

Disseminate the findings as appropriate.

Questions: Closed and Open

We turn now to a discussion of the relative merits of closed and open questions when used in either questionnaire or interview studies. In closed questions the choice of answers possible has been severely restricted by the question writer; during data analysis answers outside this array are not normally considered. The most common type of closed questions are as follows.

- Those which require yes/no or agree/disagree answers; that is, select one answer from two possible responses, although a third, 'not sure', may be added.
- Likert-style questions in which respondents are required to select one answer from a predetermined number of answers (usually an odd number, most frequently five). Each answer represents a discrete point along what has been taken by the question writer to be a continuous dependent variable, eg strongly agree, agree, neutral (neither agree nor disagree), disagree, strongly disagree. (For more information about this type of question see Ashcroft *et al.*, 1996, and Anderson, 1990). One outcome which is measured quite frequently using a Likert-style approach is student overall satisfaction with a course or course component. If you decide to use Likert-type questions to measure student satisfaction or enjoyment, you need to be aware of a tendency for respondents to tick the middle box (in this case neither satisfied nor dissatisfied). Even more annoyingly, some respondents feel a strong need to tick in between boxes.
- Multiple-choice questions in which respondents select answers (usually just one) from a number (usually at least four) of alternatives called 'distracters'. Although similar to Likert-type questions as far as respondents are concerned, multiple-choice questions differ in their construction since the distracters taken together do not represent discrete points along a single continuous dependent variable.
- Multiple-choice questions, similar in construction to those mentioned above, but different in that instead of ticking just one response, respondents are required to rank alternatives according to a criterion specified in the question. Respondents could be asked to rank all five (say) alternatives, or they could be asked to select the five most important answers from a much larger array and then to rank their chosen five according to importance. Students could be asked to rank in order of effectiveness the

methods of learning employed on their course; for example, seminars, lectures, peer presentations, educational software, visiting speakers, workplace learning, videos, self-study packs, etc. Equally, students could be asked to rank in order of importance the aims of the assessment programme for the course they are on.

Owing to the nature of the type of evaluation studies that you are most likely to be undertaking, we would suggest that using an interview approach to ask closed questions is not an effective use of the research time that you have managed to secure for yourself; closed questions are handled much more effectively via questionnaires. You might like to investigate whether different styles of questions affect the quality of the evaluative information obtained. You might also like to undertake an evaluation of any conclusions that you come to in the light of the following discussion.

From a respondent's perspective, closed questions are quick and easy to complete and, provided that you don't ask too many questions (we have seen some multiple-choice questionnaires that have been over 20 closely typed pages in length!), people, by and large, respond readily to this type of exercise. From the researcher's point of view, closed questions are unlikely to prove rich sources of data: you don't discover any new categories, just the proportions of people selecting the various distracters; however, data are easy to collate and quick to analyse. Closed questions can be annoying to those respondents who want to add some elaboration of their own to a simple yes/no question, and to those respondents who want to add an extra distracter to a multiple-choice question. In this latter situation, inclusion of 'none of these' may help respondents, but it offers little by way of informing you as to what such people do think. When using Likert-type questions you may need to bear in mind that some people, even if given seven points to choose from, will still want to tick in the space between two of the points provided! Although it is a relatively simple matter to restrict answers so as to be acceptable to you, it is quite another matter to constrain people to selecting only those answers.

Unfortunately, because you are not able to categorize in a meaningful way responses which don't conform to what is required, they usually have to be disregarded: for the purposes of data analysis, non-conforming responses are treated in the same way as a non-response.

Open-ended questions may offer the facility of finding out more about what respondents really think, provided they are willing to divulge to you their deeply held beliefs and opinions, but this is not always the case. Instead of the several lines of answer which you were expecting, all you may receive is a minimal response – a very short, little thought through, phrase or statement. Although the person has responded to the question, they have done so half-heartedly. Furthermore, there is the danger, especially for the beginning researcher, of constructing what appears to be open questions but which, since they lead respondents to one type of answer, are in reality best considered as 'closed'. For example, 'In what ways has my course of lectures enabled you to become a more semi-autonomous learner?', may seem, when taken at face value to be an open question but it does assume that answers will affirm the underlying belief, that is, that your lectures have had a positive effect on students' self autonomy. A further point to consider is that although open questions have the potential to provide quite rich data, these data, once collected, can be very time-consuming to collate and analyse, especially if you have multiple sources of data. As mentioned earlier, Maykut and Morehouse (1994) describe in some detail a technique, called the 'constant comparative method', by which qualitative and non-categorical data may be analysed.

Now that we have considered the strengths and weaknesses of open and closed questions, and how these different types of questions may be included in questionnaire and interview studies, the following research task describes the various steps which need to be considered whenever you decide to undertake an evaluation of your teaching using either questionnaire or interview approaches. Only brief details will be provided here since the processes and procedures are similar to those described in the previous research task.

RESEARCH TASK. EVALUATING A PROGRAMME OF STUDY

Choose a series of sessions that you have just taught and which comprise a coherent whole (at least six sessions will be necessary to make the task meaningful).

You will need to consider:

- your reasons for wanting to undertake this evaluation; for example, do you want to find out students' perceptions of the effectiveness of your general teaching, or whether or not the group practical tasks that you set have had the desired, but non-assessed, learning outcomes? These reasons will need to be kept in mind throughout all the steps that follow;
- what information you will need to collect so that you can address the reasons identified already;

- what methods – eg, interview, questionnaire – you will use to collect this information;
- who – eg, students, ex-students, employers – you will collect the necessary information from;
- how you will analyse and evaluate the information you have collected;
- how, and to whom, you will report any conclusions that you eventually come to.

Document Analysis

Document analysis, and in particular the analysis of student diaries and learning logs, can provide the lecturer-cum-researcher with a very rich and varied source of evaluation data. Learning logs can be used to provide data for two (at least) quite different purposes and it is important to remember that these purposes can, if not managed sensitively, cause a conflict of interest for students. Learning logs can be used as a means of obtaining the evidence necessary to enable you to undertake formative assessments of students' ongoing development of cognitive and analytical skills, as well as to chart students' learning overall (summative assessment). Learning logs can also be used as a prime source of ongoing evaluation data. These two purposes, although quite distinct, are often confounded in the classroom. Students complete their learning log as part of the work required for their course, but the lecturer concerned, in addition and with the agreement of students, uses the data provided for evaluative/research purposes. However, any material that you might suggest students include in a learning log which is to be used for research purposes may well be quite different from the material they might wish to include in a log to be used for assessment purposes only. Also, in the latter situation students have to complete their log as part of their course work whereas in the former situation they undertake the work as a volunteer. If students are volunteers they need to be able to see the benefits that are likely to accrue to either themselves or future students as a consequence of undertaking this work; if they cannot identify and justify the benefits they may lose interest and provide you with data that are of little use. As far as the quality of your research is concerned, let alone any ethical considerations, students will need prior information concerning the reasons for compiling a learning log.

Even if students are informed right from the start that their log is to be used for course or component evaluation purposes they may still need help in completing the task. In particular, students will need to know:

- how often they are expected to provide a log entry; for example, whether they are expected to complete an entry when something of significance occurs or whether they are expected to complete an entry at points in the course specified by you;
- where the focus for the evaluation lies; for example, whether it is on the teaching (input-focused evaluation), whether it is on how, and in which contexts, the learning has taken place (process-focused evaluation), or whether the focus is on what students feel they have actually learnt (outcome-focused evaluation);
- what teaching/learning situations count for evaluation purposes, for instance, formal (classroom-based) only; formal and informal (for example, private reading and work in the library); work-based experiences; academic only; both institution and work-based learning;
- how to complete a log entry – what is being looked for (criteria for selection) and the level of detail expected. In terms of the quality of your research, it is worth remembering that students who have had prior experience of writing reflective/evaluative journals are more likely to produce the most perceptive data.

Other documents which may provide you with useful contextualizing or comparative data include:

- previous course or component evaluations and reports;
- reports from external examiners and the responses from teaching teams;
- promotional material sent out to applicants, etc;
- reports to external bodies, such as course review documents to validating bodies and institutional self-evaluations;
- reports from external bodies – validating/accrediting bodies, inspectors/assessors acting on behalf of central government and other funding agencies, for example in England, OFSTED and Funding Councils.

Apart from providing contextualizing information, documents of the type mentioned above can provide invaluable data for use in longitudinal studies, for example investigating how student perceptions have changed over a five-year period, or how employer concerns regarding the relevance of a course have been modified as a result of changes to the course. You might like to investigate how student diaries may be used for purposes of component evaluation, and whether or not conflict of student interests occurs if diaries are used for both assessment and evaluation purposes.

RESEARCH TASK. ANALYSING CRITERIA USED IN EVALUATION REPORTS

Look at internally or externally produced evaluation reports covering several institutions. Analyse the implied criteria for quality being used by those writing the reports relating to some of the features below (adapted from Higher Education Quality Council, 1994):

Entry to the institution:
admissions policies;
admissions requirements;
information for prospective students;
pre-entry guidance;
the selection process;
facilitating student entry.

The quality of the student experience:
quality assurance processes;
choice and diversity;
programme approval;
programme information for students;
teaching;
learning;
evaluation of programmes of study;
evaluation of teaching and learning;
quality enhancement systems;
staff appointment;
staff development and training;
staff appraisal;
collaborative arrangements with other institutions;
student support services;
student grievance systems.

Student outcomes:
student progress;
student assessment;
qualifications gained;
verification of standards.

Undertake an analysis of:
the number of statements in each report relating to particular features;
the content of such statements;
words and phases that reoccur.

Consider whether the emerging criteria serve bureaucratic, political or developmental purposes.

Discuss and adapt your analysis with an experienced colleague.

Write a paper that discusses the compatibility of criteria for success used by certain parts of the educational system with the interests of various stakeholders in education.

Using Observation to Collect Data for Evaluative Purposes

In this final part of the discussion of techniques for the collection of evaluation data, we will outline two approaches to observation which, in the main, may be distinguished one from the other by the role adopted by the observer. In the first approach, called participant observation, the observer is an integral part of the situation being studied; in the second, called non-participant observation, the observer is outside the process and so, metaphorically speaking, is an outsider looking into the situation being studied.

When using either questionnaires or interviews to collect data from students, you are in fact asking them post hoc questions about their learning: in this sense you are, as was mentioned earlier, relying on students being able to trawl from their memory recollections of past events, some of which may have happened some time ago. It could be argued that this process of collecting data is highly suspect. Over time memories get distorted and perceptions change, things get forgotten, and the significance of an event may well change in the light of subsequent experience (not in itself a negative feature as far as evaluation is concerned). Observation is a method of collecting data which does not rely on memory, and so does not suffer from drawbacks of this sort.

Participant Observation

In participant observation the observer (lecturer) concerned collects first-hand data about what is taking place in their classroom at the same time as they undertake their usual teaching role. The lecturer fulfils two roles simultaneously: teacher, and observer of a situation in which they play a significant part. Since teaching is very demanding in terms of both time and personal energy, the ways in which you make observations of the learning situation and then record them have to be fairly straightforward, time-effective and easy to manage. These constraints imply that just two approaches to participant observation are possible: the unstructured approach and the semi-structured approach. (A third method, often called the structured approach, is best considered under non-participant observation and is therefore described in more detail in the next section.)

The unstructured approach involves you in recording anything which you find interesting or which you feel might be capable of providing you with the evaluative data you seek. The problem with this approach is that, although it can be very useful in the initial stages of a piece of research when you may wish to identify significant issues to be followed up in more detail, so much is going on in the classroom that unless you are selective your observations may well lack a focus and, instead of being detailed, the observations you record may be general and non-specific. The second, and perhaps more manageable, way forward is to adopt a semi-structured approach. Here, instead of having a blank sheet of paper at the beginning of your period of observation, you start off with a number of categories (perhaps identified from experience or through a period of unstructured observation) around which you want to collect data.

Clearly, the categories you identify as being of relevance will relate to the purposes for the observations that are made, and these in turn are likely to be linked to the aims and objectives of the situations being observed. To help you get started, listed below are some broad headings which you could use as a basis for formulating categories of your own:

- what students say, to one another and to you, and the responses that this generates; for example, you could concentrate on the types of questions students ask;
- what students do; for example, how they interact during group discussion work, how they, either individually or in groups, perform a presentation task that you have set.

Given the demands of teaching and observing for research purposes, rather than attempt to observe a whole session you may find it more appropriate to concentrate on a very small and discrete section of it (such as group discussion work) which is linked closely to your overall purpose.

Even using the semi-structured approach, the observations which you make, because the whole process needs to be manageable within the confines of your day-to-day teaching, are likely to be relatively informal; you take note of something because it stands apart from everything else that is going on at the time. However, it is important to bear in mind that observation is to do with collecting information using all the senses, not simply sight. What students say therefore forms an important data source. Analysis arising out of data collected using this informal, non-systematic form of observation may lead you to some tentative, yet interesting, conclusions concerning what happens, or does not happen, during your sessions. You may want to explore the issues which emerge more fully through a more systematic form of observation, perhaps using an observation schedule; how to do this is discussed in the next section.

Non-participant Observation

In this approach, someone outside the context of your normal teaching-learning situation (this could be a colleague), is invited into your classroom for the purposes of making observations. One form of non-participant observation occurs when an institutional appraiser, or an appraiser/inspector from outside your institution, visits your classroom for the purposes of collecting data for evaluation purposes. Here the agenda which the visitor brings with her or him is likely to be external to your normal work situation, and the criteria for the selection of observational data may not be of your choosing. If you work in England, either in the further education sector or in certain other sections of higher education, this non-participant approach to the collection of data is unlikely to be new to you. You may be quite used to receiving visitors from a Funding Council or from OFSTED; equally, you may feel that having outsiders observe your classroom is a threatening development in your teaching.

The direction we wish to consider in this section is, however, towards informal approaches to non-participant observation, such as that conducted by colleagues internal to your department or faculty, and not on more formal approaches undertaken by managers or outsiders for purposes such as staff appraisal or the generation of institutional performance indicators. Having said that, you may wish to undertake a comparison of the validity of internally and externally generated observation categories and the reliability of the data collected using these categories. For instance, you might investigate whether or not external comparisons are high on reliability but low on validity and whether the reverse is true of data collected using categories generated via internal mechanisms.

The non-participant form of observation is appropriate to all three approaches mentioned earlier, but since the unstructured and semi-structured approaches have been described already, in this section we shall confine the discussion to the structured approach to observation.

At the heart of the structured approach lies the observation schedule. The detail of the schedule (the observations to be made) will, clearly, be determined by the nature of the issues and the situations through which these issues are explored. For example, a schedule for investigating how students devote their time during sessions is likely to elicit different observations than a schedule investigating the different types of questions students ask; exploring how students spend their time during tightly structured classroom-based tasks is likely to require a different schedule than if the observations were to take place during a science practical class.

Many observation schedules use a grid format: down the left-hand side, written out as a list, is a series of statements which when taken together define the domain (activities relevant to the area of teaching/learning) being studied. The remainder of the page is given over to a series of columns which divide up into a number of time periods, for example every five seconds or every 30 seconds, that part of the session being observed. At the end of each time period – not during – the observer ticks the relevant cell (activity statement in respect of the targeted student(s) against time period) on the grid. When completed, the schedule can be used to recreate how the targeted students spent their time during the period of observation. To ensure that the task is manageable, the number of students studied may need to be restricted to only one or two, if they are working individually (a separate schedule needs to be kept for each student), or, if working collaboratively, one group considered as a single entity.

Clearly, the usefulness of the schedule relies, in part, on the extent to which the observation statements, taken as a whole, describe the domain being studied. Therefore, pilot work is essential to ensure that the list of statements describes comprehensively and exclusively the domain in question.

Taking one of the examples cited above – how students spend their time during practical work – an observation schedule might be divided into:

- task-related activities,
- non-task-related activities, and
- other activities.

Task-related activities might include: reading from a textbook, completing a competence pro forma, using a machine as instructed, completing a report in a practical file, seeking clarification from you concerning the exact nature of the task which you have set, etc. Non-task activities might include: talking with another student about an out-of-class activity, writing down a friend's telephone number, looking out of the window. Activities such as going to the toilet, doodling on a piece of paper while waiting for you to answer a task-related query, standing up to allow their neighbour to get back to their seat, you may want to classify as 'other'.

Having read the list of activities in the previous paragraph, you've probably come to the conclusion that there are many activities which cannot be assigned unambiguously. For example, you might decide that a student who is waiting to talk with you should be classified as on task:

however, in the case of other activities it is much more difficult to make an assignment with any degree of certainty. The student who is looking out of the window may be thinking about what to write next: equally, they may be thinking about what to eat for lunch. Even though you cannot be sure, the important thing is to be consistent; for example, unless there is evidence to the contrary, you might decide to categorize all window-gazing as off task.

Despite the potential for ambiguity, the use of observation schedules by non-participant observers was particularly common before video cameras became fairly readily available for use in classrooms. Therefore, why not investigate how a video camera might be used to help you observe and reflect on your own teaching? After all, constructing an appropriate observation schedule is a relatively straightforward task; completing one yourself during a lesson is quite another. Using a video camera to help you reflect on your own teaching in a way which is more distanced and objective than if you tried to do this during a session does have the advantage that, as the participant observer, you know your students better than any non-participant observer ever could, and so any assignments you make may be nearer to the truth. In effect you would be coupling the reliability benefits of non-participatory observation with the level of validity accorded to a participatory style of data collection, analysis and interpretation.

If you are not able, for whatever reason, to use a video camera, why not enlist the help of a colleague? You could undertake a piece of collaborative research where she or he completes observation schedules on a number of your sessions and you complete schedules in respect of sessions which she or he teaches. If you then want to use the two sets of schedules for purposes of comparison you will need to make sure that what is known as inter-observer reliability (both of you agree consistently on the category to which single observations are to be assigned) is as high as possible. Achieving this level of reliability requires time to come to a common understanding: to achieve this both of you could observe the same lessons of colleagues with each of you completing schedules separately and discussing them together afterwards. Alternatively, if you do have access to a video camera, but prefer to undertake an evaluation of your teaching as part of a collaborative project, then you could investigate how videos of sessions, including those made by other people, might help in coming to a better shared understanding of how specific observations are to be coded. The research task which follows asks you to evaluate systematically either your own teaching or that of a colleague.

RESEARCH TASK. OBSERVATION OF TEACHING AS AN EVALUATION METHOD

Identify the reasons why you want to observe your teaching using any of the approaches mentioned above. This process should help you sharpen the focus for your study, identify which students might be asked to participate, and also provide boundaries which determine the start and end point of each period of observation. The focus for the observations might be:

- how you divide your time between groups during group work;
- the types of open questions during seminar or tutorial work;
- how personal characteristics affect the quality of group discussions.

Decide whether you want to undertake the work on your own or with a colleague: are there any colleagues who could collaborate with you?

Decide on a draft observation schedule for the analysis of the activities to be observed. Consult relevant textbooks and journal articles.

Refine the draft schedule by using it to analyse activities, either from a video recording of one of your sessions or from first-hand observation of a colleague's session. Don't forget to ask students for permission to record them on video and to use the video for research purposes.

Check for the validity of the final schedule. Ask:

- Does the schedule appear to be addressing the issues you intended?
- Does the schedule look right from a professional point of view?

Undertake agreement trials: either discuss with a colleague your assignment of the events which took place on the video recording, or discuss with your collaborator the assignment of events which occurred during observation of one another's sessions. If you are working by yourself, getting a colleague to help validate your observation schedule and the conclusions you come to based on it may be difficult. However, if you are considering writing up your work for external publication, it is desirable, even essential, that you do this: validate your work now, it's too late to do so when you start to write up. Agree the final framework for analysis based upon this process of validation.

Complete your observations of the designated activities and/or students. What steps have you taken to ensure that the behaviours you observe are typical? For example, how sure are you that students are not 'playing to the camera'? Analyse the data and, if you are working alone, ask a colleague to check on the validity of your final conclusions.

Act upon the results as appropriate to your work situation and to your department or institution.

Now begin the process of writing up for publication the work you have completed during this research task. In describing what you have done and the conclusions that you have reached, don't forget to mention the steps you took to validate you work. If you're not sure how to write this article, refer back to the first research task in this chapter.

Annotated Reading List

Balla, J and Boyle, P (1994) 'Assessment of student performance: a framework for improving practice', *Assessment and Evaluation in Higher Education*, 19, 1, 7–28.

In this paper the authors put forward the point that although much is known about assessment which has the potential to inform good practice, change in practice is very slow. With this in mind a model is outlined for quality management in evaluation.

Taylor, L (1994) 'Reflecting on teaching: the benefits of self- evaluation', *Assessment and Evaluation in Higher Education*, 19, 2, 109–22.

A comprehensive paper containing many suggestions including some relating to peer assessment. A technique for lecturer self-evaluation which the author has found to be successful is described.

Willmot, M and McLean, M (1994) 'Evaluating flexible learning: a case study', *Journal of Further and Higher Education*, 18, 3, 99–108.

This paper presents a very good model, based on a research and development approach to institutional self-evaluation, for you to apply to the evaluation of your own courses.

References

Anderson, G (1990) *Fundamentals of Educational Research*, London: Falmer Press.

Ashcroft, K, Bigger, S and Coates, D (1996) *Researching into Equal Opportunities in Colleges and Universities*, London: Kogan Page.

Bell, J (1993) *Doing Your Research Project*, 2nd edn, Buckingham: Open University Press.

Bennett, C, Higgins, C and Foreman-Peck, L (1996) *Researching into Teaching Methods in Colleges and Universities*, London: Kogan Page.

Bennett, S, Bigger, S, Ngeh, J and Yuriev, E (1995) 'HELPA: a rapid means of student evaluation of lecturing performance in higher education', *Assessment and Evaluation in Higher Education*, 20, 2, 191–202.

Bonetti, S (1994) 'On the use of student questionnaires', *Higher Education Review*, 26, 3, 57–64.

Cohen, L and Manion, L (1994) *Research Methods in Education*, 4th edn, London: Routledge.

Higher Education Quality Council (1994) *A Briefing Paper from the Higher Education Quality Council: Checklist for quality assurance systems*, London: HEQC.

Hopkins, D (1993) *A Teacher's Guide to Classroom Research*, 2nd edn, Buckingham: Open University Press.

Maykut, P and Morehouse, R (1994) *Beginning Qualitative Research. A philosophic and practical guide*, London: Falmer Press.

Williams, E (1992) 'Student attitudes towards approaches to learning and assessment', *Assessment and Evaluation in Higher Education*, 17, 1, 45–58.

Chapter 8

Series Conclusion: Getting Published

Kate Ashcroft

Books from the Publisher's Point of View

Getting started on writing a book is often the hardest part of the process. You need to convince yourself that the things that you know about and that interest you will matter sufficiently to other people to make publication worthwhile, and then you have to get down to it. In choosing a topic for a book, there is always a balance to be struck between your needs and those of the reader. For example, you may have completed a research degree in the area of assessment or evaluation within science courses, and found the subject of your dissertation interesting. However, it is likely to require a complete rewrite and reorientation of the way you approach the subject before it becomes interesting to a larger group of readers.

Publishers receive much unsolicited material through the mail, often in the form of a covering letter and some 'finished' material. Most will consider such approaches carefully. Even so, this is likely to be the least productive way of approaching a publisher. The highest 'hit' rate is likely to be achieved if you are invited to put a proposal forward. Such invitations rarely happen by accident. They often result from putting yourself in the right place at the right time. To do this, you may need to develop networks of contacts. Commissioning editors get to know about potential authors through a number of routes. They attend conferences: you can meet them there and talk to them about your specialist area. They ask influential groups and individuals about likely authors when they perceive a niche in the market: you might get to know the committee members of relevant associations and make sure they know about your potential contribution. They often ask established writers to contribute to book series. These 'names' often already have sufficient commissions. If you can get to know established authors, and ensure that they know about you and your interests, they may suggest your name to the editor instead. Commissioning editors also read the educational press: not so much learned journals as papers such as *The Times Educational Supplement, The Times Higher Educational Supplement* and *Education.* If you have written for such papers, your name may become known in the right circles.

Editors also look for pockets of good practice and investigate them for potential authors. If your institution has had an excellent inspection report, or if you are a member of a consortium of colleges or universities that share good practice, you do not have to wait to be discovered. It may be worth drawing an editor's attention to what you are doing and to invite them to talk to you and others about its publishing potential.

I have to admit to never having acted in the ways described above. I received commissions the hard way: by putting a good quality submission to an appropriate publisher. I have been successful when I looked at the process from the editor's point of view. The publisher is much more interested in their readers' needs, and in making a profit, than in your interests. If you can present what you want to do in these terms, you may be successful. This is likely to require some research to find out who your readers are likely to be, how many of them there are, where they will be found, what their interests are and why they will want to buy your particular book.

The publisher will also be interested in the competition for the book you are proposing. If you tell him or her that there is no competition, you are likely to be asked to do more research. If you still cannot find books on your subject, the publisher may worry that there is a good reason why nobody else is publishing in that area. You may be more successful if you undertake a thorough trawl of other publications on topics related to the one that you wish to write about, and then think clearly about your particular selling points and how you can make your book better than the others on the market. Your arguments may vary, depending on what you are writing about. When I co-edited a book on the new National Curriculum, we sold it on the fact that it would be particularly timely (it was to be the first book after the new Orders were published). When I wrote a book on quality and standards, I made sure that it looked at quality issues from the lecturer's point of view (others mainly wrote for institutional managers).

Choosing a Publisher

Once you are clear about what you intend to write and who you are writing for, you will need to choose a publisher. In the UK, there are a relatively small number of publishing houses that specialize in books about education and that are interested in publishing material about further and higher education in particular. Most of the main ones feature in the list of publishers towards the end of this chapter. In addition, there are a number of publishers who are based in other countries and a number of universities have developed their own small in-house publishing companies.

A few academic authors use a literary agent. If you wish to do so, the *Artists and Writers Year Book* will help you locate an appropriate one. If you decide to go it alone, you may find it useful to look around at the book lists of various publishers to find those that have a sizeable list in your subject. It is easier to market a group of books with a common theme. If a publisher is advertising a book series in the area of assessment or evaluation, they may be more likely to look seriously at your proposal. The next stage is to look at publishers' house-styles: the appearance of the books, the type of print and layout, and the usual length and format of the books they produce. You will also have to decide whether to go for a large publishing house or a smaller, more specialized one. Larger houses have the marketing facilities to promote books across the world. On the other hand, junior editors in large houses have little power and may take some time to get approval for action. Small publishing houses may give more personal service. They also tend to be more highly specialized and so know a lot about publishing in a particular field.

Negotiating the Contract

Once it looks like you are more or less 'in business', you will need to discuss terms and conditions. The level of royalties offered by academic publishers does not vary greatly, but it is always worth trying to negotiate a slightly better deal or asking for a small advance on royalties, especially if you are involved in some immediate expenses. Whatever terms you eventually agree, it is important to read your contract carefully. Most are fairly standard. You may be paid royalties as a percentage of the net price. On the other hand, especially if your book is the type that may be sold at a discount (for instance, through book clubs), your royalties may be a percentage of net receipts (what the publishing house actually receives from sales). This arrangement allows the publisher to pay you a lower amount per book sold, where the books are sold at a discount. If you are editing a book with chapters contributed by others, the publishing house may pay the chapter authors a small fee on publication. The total of these fees may then be set against your royalties.

Copyright may be held by the publisher or the author. In practice, this may make little difference, as, in any case, the publisher will normally reserve exclusive publishing rights. In other cases the small print on contracts can be important. For instance, I would never sign a contract that gave the publisher an option on subsequent books.

Your contract is likely to say that the publisher reserves the right not to publish your book if you deliver it after a fixed date or if it is of poor quality. In practice, these clauses are not often invoked. Provided you have let your editor know in advance of the deadline, she or he will usually be willing to allow some slippage. If it does not come up to expectations, she or he will also usually help you to improve the book, rather than abandon it altogether. There will usually be a clause in the contract about excess correction charges.

It is in your interests to undertake careful proof-reading at the early stages. Once the book has been typeset, substantial changes late in the process can have knock-on effects you may not have anticipated: for instance, the indexing may need to be redone. Do not forget to check the spelling on the title pages. I have heard of a spelling mistake that was found on the cover after binding; as a consequence, the author lost several hundred pounds in royalties.

One decision you will have to make is whether to do your own indexing. Most publishers have links with professional indexers who will do this job for you for a charge that is set against royalties. Professional indexers usually do a sound job, but they may not know the subject area as well you do. If you decide to do your own index, your editor should be able to provide you with guidelines on house-style and give you tips to make the job relatively painless (for instance, using a highlighter on a photocopy at the proof-reading stage to mark significant words and phrases). Indexing computer programs exist that can simplify the job a little.

Your relationship with your editor is likely to develop over time. Many authors stick with one editor over a considerable period. This relationship will be much easier if you are the sort of person who meets deadlines. Your editor is more likely to work hard on behalf of a cooperative and efficient author who answers correspondence promptly and delivers on time. Because the unexpected always occurs, I always aim to complete the book well before the agreed deadline.

The process of checking references, tidying headings, creating the table of contents and so on takes a lot of time. When you submit the manuscript, you need to be prepared for more work. The publisher may send you a marked-up manuscript to check before typesetting. If so, it is important that you have set aside the time to do a thorough job. This will be the last chance to make substantial changes. After the manuscript has been typeset, you will be asked to undertake thorough and careful proof-reading. At the same time, it is likely that you will be approached by the marketing department with requests for a range of information to help the publisher to sell the book. This is an important stage, and one to which you should give time and thought. It is probably a good idea to talk through the post-submission schedule with your publisher, so that you can blank out some days in your diary to do all this work.

The marketing of your book is partially your responsibility. The low profit margin on academic books means that your book is unlikely to be advertised in the press (unless it is part of a series that may be included in a composite advertisement). A few books will be sent out for review. If you expect to see your book described in the educational press during the following months, you may be disappointed. Not all books sent for review will be included and, even where they are, the review may not be printed for up to a year. Much marketing takes place through direct mail shots. The publicity department will need your help in targeting these. Another important marketing outlet is the conference circuit. You will need to inform the marketing department of key events where publicity about your book should be available. If you are giving a paper at a conference, you should make sure that your book is on prominent display. Do not be afraid to act as a shameless self-publicist.

Writing for a Journal

The most usual way of getting started in publishing is to write for a newspaper or journal. If you submit articles for the educational press, you will be up against stiff competition from professional journalists. Unless you have already established a name within education, you may find it is a difficult field to break into. You may be more likely to succeed if your article has something special that will catch the editor's attention. On the whole, the educational press wants interesting articles, written in a short and non-technical way. It may not be interested in straightforward research reports.

You are unlikely to be paid for a paper or article in a journal, but this form of publishing can make a good starting point for a would-be academic author. Once you have completed your thinking, reading, research and/or enquiry, ideally you should start to consider the journals that might accept it before you start writing so that you can adapt your style to their requirements.

On the whole, you will achieve more status and professional recognition if you publish in a refereed journal, especially if it reaches an international audience. The refereeing process means that the quality of your paper is subjected to scrutiny by (usually two) outside experts, before it is published. They will often suggest that you should change your paper in various ways. You may want to consider these requests very seriously, since they are usually made by people who know a great deal about the subject and about writing. On the other hand, the paper is yours, and you may decide not to agree to changes if that would make the paper say things that you disagree with or fundamentally change the tone you wished to take.

More status is accorded to publication in very well-established journals. On the other hand, they tend to have a large number of experienced writers who regularly write for them: your paper will compete for space with many experts. You may stand a better chance of being published if you submit to a relatively new publication. My first paper appeared in the (then) new international journal *Assessment and Evaluation in Higher Education* that has now grown into a very well respected publication. If you start with a new journal, and if you both do well, you can build a long-lasting relationship to your mutual benefit.

The frequency of publication may be another factor in your choice of journal. Journals that only appear once or twice a year may not deal with your paper expeditiously. Since it is generally not 'done' to send your paper to several journals at the same time, this can be a real problem. A journal that publishes more regularly will probably referee and publish your paper more quickly. This is especially important if your paper is on a topical theme.

You will find detailed guidance at the back of most journals on how the editors need you to set out your manuscript, references and so on. It will generally explain the usual length of acceptable articles and the number of copies of the manuscript that must be sent. It is important to keep to these guidelines.

List of Educational Publishers

Details of the policies of many of the publishers and journals below may be found in Bennett, Higgins and Foreman-Peck *Researching into Teaching Methods in Colleges and Universities* (1996), the companion book to this in the Practical Research Series.

Cassell, Wellington House, 125 Strand, London WC2X 0BB. Telephone: 0171 420 5555.
David Fulton, 2 Barbon Close, Great Ormond Street, London WC1N 3JX.
   Telephone: 0171 405 5656.
Falmer Press, 4 John Street, London WC1N 2ET. Telephone: 0171 405 2237.
Framework Press, Parkfield, Greaves Road, Lancaster LA1 4TZ. Telephone: 01524 39602.
Further Education Development Agency, Publications Department, Coombe Lodge,
   Blagdon, Bristol BS18 6RG. Telephone: 01761 462503.
Heinemann, Halley Court, Jordan Hill, Oxford OX2 8EJ. Telephone: 01865 311366.
Hodder & Stoughton, 338 Euston Road, London NW1 3BH. Telephone: 0171 873 6000.
Jessica Kingsley, 116 Pentonville Road, London N1 9JB. Telephone: 0171 833 2307.
Kogan Page, 120 Pentonville Road, London N1 9JN. Telephone: 0171 278 0433.
Macmillan, Brunel Road, Houndsmills, Basingstoke RG21 2XS. Telephone: 01256 29242.
Open University Press, Cedric Court, 22 Billmoor, Buckingham MK18 1XW.
   Telephone: 01280 823388.
Oxford University Press, Walton Street, Oxford OX2 6DP. Telephone: 01865 56767.
Pergamon Press, Elsevier Science Ltd, The Boulevard, Langford Lane, Kidlington
   OX5 1GB. Telephone: 01865 843000.
Routledge, 11 New Fetter Lane, London EC4P 4EE. Telephone: 0171 583 9855.
Scottish Academic Press, 56 Hanover Street, Edinburgh EH2 2DX.
   Telephone: 0131 255 7483.
Staff and Educational Development Association, Gala House, 3 Raglan Road, Edgbaston,
   Birmingham B5 7RA. Telephone: 0121 4405021.

Other Publishers with Education-related Lists

Lawrence Erlbaum, 27 Church Road, Hove, East Sussex BN3 2FA.
HMSO, PO Box 276, London SW8 5DT.
International Reading Association, 800 Barksdale Road, PO Box 8139, Newark,
   DE 1914-8139, USA.
JAI Press, 55 Old Post Road, Number 2, PO Box 1678, Greenwich, Connecticut 06836-1678,
   USA.
Multilingual Matters, Frankfurt Lodge, Clevedon Hall, Victoria Road, Clevedon BS21 7SJ.
NATE, 50 Broadfield Road, Broadfield Business Centre, Sheffield S8 0XJ.
Nelson, ITPS, North Way, Andover SP10 5BR.
Pitman, 12–14 Slaidburn Crescent, Southport, Merseyside PR9 7BR.
Plenum, 233 Spring Street, New York, NY 10013-1578, USA.
Policy Studies Institute, 100 Park Village East, London NW1 3S.
Technical and Educational Services, Ravenswood Road, Bristol BS6 6BW.
Teachers College Press, 3 Henrietta Street, Covent Garden, London WC2E 8LU.
Trentham Books, 734 London Road, Oakhill, Stoke on Trent ST4 5NP.
Triangle Books, PO Box 65, Wallingford, Oxon OX10 0YG.

List of Educational Journals

Assessment and Evaluation in Higher Education
Carfax. Published three times a year.
Manuscripts to: WAH Scott, School of Education, University of Bath, Bath BA2 7AY.
This established refereed journal welcomes pragmatic research-based or reflective studies which help to illuminate everyday practice. The research that is published is not necessarily large scale, but it tends to be good of its kind.

Assessment in Education: Principles, Policy and Practice
Carfax. Published three times a year.
Manuscripts to: P Broadfoot, School of Education, University of Bristol, Helen Woodhouse Building, 35 Berkley Square, Bristol BS8 1JA.
This new international refereed journal is interested in papers that compare assessment policy and practice between settings, detailed case studies and other forms of research.

Quality Assurance in Education
MCB University Press. Published three times a year.
Manuscripts to: G McElwee, School of Management, University of Humberside, Cottingham Road, Hull HU6 7RT.
This fairly new international journal is looking for short papers that critically examine quality-related issues in education and bridge the theory/practice divide, including real-life case studies and examples of standards for, and measurements of, quality levels.

Quality in Higher Education
Carfax. Published three times a year.
Manuscripts to: L Harvey, Centre for Research into Quality, Baker Building, University of Central England, Franchise Street, Perry Barr, Birmingham B42 2SU.
This new journal is aimed at those interested in the theory, policy and practice of quality control, management and improvement within higher education. The papers include carefully reasoned debate about these issues, supported by an analysis of the international literature.

British Educational Research Journal
Carfax. Published quarterly.
Manuscripts to: G Weiner, Department of Education, South Bank University, London.

British Journal of Educational Studies
Blackwell. Published quarterly.
Manuscripts to: D Halpin, University of Warwick, Coventry.

Cambridge Journal of Education
Triangle. Published three times a year.
Manuscripts to: B Shannon, University of Cambridge Institute of Education.

Education Today
Pitman. Published quarterly.
Manuscripts to: The Editor, College of Preceptors, Coppice Row, Theydon Bois, Epping.

Educational Research
Routledge. Published three time a year.
Manuscripts to: S Hegarty, National Foundation for Educational Research, The Mere, Upton Park, Slough.

Educational Action Research
Triangle. Published three times a year.
Manuscripts to: Dr B Somekh, University of East Anglia, Norwich.

Educational Review
Carfax. Published three times a year.
Manuscripts to: Editors, University of Birmingham.

Educational Studies
Carfax. Published three times a year.
Manuscripts to: D Cherrington, Cheltenham and Gloucester College of Higher Education, Cheltenham.

Evaluation and Research in Education
Multilingual Matters. Published three times a year.
Manuscripts to: K Morrison, University of Durham.
Evaluation Practice
JAI Press. Published three times a year.
Manuscripts to: M Smith, 2115 Symons Hall, University of Maryland, College Park, MD 20742, USA.
Higher Education Policy
Kogan Page. Published quarterly.
Manuscripts to: International Association of Universities, Unesco House, 1 rue Miollis, 75732 Paris Cedex 15, France.
Higher Education Quarterly
Blackwells. Published quarterly.
Manuscripts to: M Shattock, University of Warwick, Coventry.
Higher Education Review
Tyrrell Burgess Associates. Published three times a year.
Manuscripts to: J Pratt, 46 Merers Road, London.
Innovation and Learning in Education: The International Journal for the Reflective Practitioner
MCB University Press. Published three times a year.
Manuscripts to: G McElwee, University of Humberside, Hull.
Interchange
Kluwer Academic Press. Published three times a year.
Manuscripts to: L Lenz, Faculty of Education, University of Calgary, 2500 University Drive NW, Toronto, Ontario T2N 1N4, Canada.
Journal of Education for Teaching
Carfax. Published three times a year.
Manuscripts to: E Stones, 11 Serpentine Road, Selly Park, Birmingham B29 7HU.
Journal of Further and Higher Education
NATFHE. Published three times a year.
Manuscripts to: A Castling, c/o NATFHE, 27 Britannia Street, London WC1X 9JP.
New Academic
SEDA. Published three times a year.
Manuscripts to: E Mapstone, St Yse, St Nectan's Glen, Tintagel, Cornwall PL34 OBE.
Oxford Review of Education
Carfax. Published three times a year.
Manuscripts to: D Phillips, University of Oxford Department of Educational Studies.
Qualitative Studies in Education
Taylor and Francis. Published four times a year.
Manuscripts to: S Ball, King's College London.
Research Papers in Education
Routledge. Published three times a year.
Manuscripts to: P Preece, University of Exeter.
Studies in Educational Evaluation
Pergamon. Published quarterly.
Manuscripts to: A Lewy, School of Education, Tel Aviv University, Tel Aviv.
Studies in Higher Education
Society for Research into Higher Education/Carfax. Published quarterly.
Manuscripts to: R Barnett, Institute of Education, London.
Teachers and Teaching: Theory and Practice
Carfax. Published three times a year.
Manuscripts to: C Day, University of Nottingham.
Teaching in Higher Education
Carfax. Published three times a year.
Manuscripts to: L Barton, University of Sheffield.

The Vocational Aspects of Education
Triangle. Published three times a year.
Manuscripts to: B Bailey, University of Greenwich, London.
Westminster Studies in Education
Carfax. Published annually.
Manuscripts to: WH Fearon, Westminster College, Oxford.

More specialist journals include the following

Applied Behavioral Science Review
JAI Press. Published twice a year.
Manuscripts to: DW Britt, Wayne State University, USA.
Association for Learning Technology Journal
Association for Learning Technology. Published twice a year.
Manuscripts to: G Jacob, School of European Languages, University College, Swansea.
British Journal of Educational Psychology
British Psychological Society. Published quarterly.
Manuscripts to: M Youngman, School of Education, University of Nottingham, University Park, Nottingham.
British Journal of In-Service Education
Triangle. Published three times a year.
Manuscripts to: M Lee, University College of Bretton Hall, Wakefield, West Yorkshire.
British Journal of Music Education
Cambridge University Press. Published three times a year.
Manuscripts to: J Paynter, University of York, or K Swanwick, University of London Institute of Education.
British Journal of Religious Education
Alden Press. Published three times a year.
Manuscripts to: JM Hall, University of Birmingham.
British Journal of Sociology of Education
Carfax. Published quarterly.
Manuscripts to: L Barton, Division of Education, University of Sheffield.
Comparative Education
Carfax. Published three times a year.
Manuscripts to: P Broadfoot, University of Bristol.
Compare: A Journal of Comparative Education
Carfax. Published three times a year.
Manuscripts to: C Brock, University of Oxford.
Curriculum Inquiry
Blackwell. Published quarterly.
Manuscripts to: FM Connolly, The Ontario Institute for Studies in Education.
The Curriculum Journal
Routledge. Published three times a year.
Manuscripts to: M James, University of Cambridge Institute of Education.
Curriculum Studies
Triangle. Published three times a year.
Manuscripts to: W Carr, Division of Education, University of Sheffield.
Computers and Education
Pergamon. Published eight times a year.
Manuscripts to: MR Kibby, University of Strathclyde.
Disability and Society
Carfax. Published quarterly.
Manuscripts to: L Barton, Division of Education, University of Sheffield
Education Economics
Carfax. Published three times a year.
Manuscripts to: G Johnes, Lancaster University.

Educational Management and Administration
   Pitman. Published quarterly.
   Manuscripts to: P Ribbins, Centre for Education Management and Policy Studies, School of Education, University of Birmingham.
Educational Media International
   Kogan Page. Published quarterly.
   Manuscripts to: J Bell, International Council for Educational Media, c/o Kogan Page, London.
Educational Psychology
   Carfax. Published quarterly.
   Manuscripts to: R Riding, University of Birmingham.
Educational Research and Evaluation
   Swets and Zeitlinger. Published quarterly.
   Manuscripts to: BPM Creemers, GION, University of Groningen, The Netherlands.
Educational Studies in Mathematics
   Kluwer. Published four times a year.
   Manuscripts to: Kluwer, Dordrecht, The Netherlands.
Educational Theory
   University of Illinois. Published four times a year.
   Manuscripts to: NC Burbules, University of Illinois, USA.
Environmental Education Research
   Carfax. Published three times a year.
   Manuscripts to: C Oulton, University of Bath.
European Journal of Education
   Carfax. Published quarterly.
   Manuscripts to: The Editors, European Institute of Education and Social Policy, Universite de Paris.
European Journal of Engineering Education
   Carfax. Published quarterly.
   Manuscripts to: T Becher, University of Sussex.
European Journal of Special Needs
   Routledge. Published three times a year.
   Manuscripts to: S Hegarty, National Foundation for Educational Research.
European Journal of Teacher Education
   Carfax. Published three times a year.
   Manuscripts to: M Todeschini, Istituto di Pedagogia, Universita degli studii, Milan.
Forum for Promoting 3–19 Comprehensive Education
   Triangle. Published three times a year.
   Manuscripts to: N Whitbread, Beaumont Cottage, East Langton, Market Harborough.
Gender and Education
   Carfax. Published three times a year.
   Manuscripts to: C Hughes, Department of Continuing Education, University of Warwick.
Innovations in Education and Training International
   Kogan Page. Published quarterly.
   Manuscripts to: C Bell, University of Plymouth.
International Journal of Disability and Development in Education
   University of Queensland Press. Published three times a year.
   Manuscripts to: F and E Schonell, Special Education Centre, St Lucia, Australia.
International Journal of Educational Research
   Pergamon Press. Published twelve times a year.
   Manuscripts to: HJ Walberg, University of Illinois at Chicago, USA.
International Journal of Science Education
   Taylor and Francis. Published six times a year.
   Manuscripts to: JK Gilbert, University of Reading.

International Journal of Technology and Design Education
Kluwer. Published three times a year.
Manuscripts to: The Editor, Kluwer, Dordrecht, The Netherlands.
International Research in Geographical and Environmental Education
La Trobe University Press. Published twice a year.
Manuscripts to: J Lidstone, Queensland University of Technology, Australia.
International Studies in Sociology of Education
Triangle. Published twice a year.
Manuscripts to: L Barton, Division of Education, University of Sheffield.
Issues in Education: Contributions from Educational Psychology
JAI Press. Published twice a year.
Manuscripts to: J Carson, School of Education, University of California, USA.
Journal of Access Studies
Jessica Kingsley. Published twice a year,
Manuscripts to: P Jones, Higher Education Quality Council.
Journal for Educational Policy
Taylor and Francis. Published six times a year.
Manuscripts to: S Ball, King's College London.
Journal of Aesthetic Education
University of Illinois Press. Published quarterly.
Manuscripts to: University of Illinois, USA.
Journal of Art and Design Education
Blackwell. Published three times a year.
Manuscripts to: J Swift, University of Central England, Birmingham.
Journal of Biological Education
Institute of Biology. Published quarterly.
Manuscripts to: The Editor, 20–22 Queensberry Place, London.
Journal of Computer Assisted Learning
Blackwell. Published quarterly.
Manuscripts to: R Lewis, University of Lancaster.
Journal of Educational Television
Carfax. Published three times a year.
Manuscripts to: M Messenger Davies, The London Institute.
Journal of Geography in Higher Education
Carfax. Published three times a year.
Manuscripts to: M Healey, Cheltenham and Gloucester College of Higher Education.
Journal of Information Technology for Teacher Education
Triangle. Published twice a year.
Manuscripts to: B Robinson, Department of Education, University of Cambridge.
Journal of Moral Education
Carfax. Published three times a year.
Manuscripts to: MJ Taylor, National Foundation for Educational Research.
Journal of Open and Distance Learning
Open University/Pitman. Published three times a year.
Manuscripts to: J Matthews, Regional Academic Services, The Open University.
Journal of Philosophy of Education
Redwood Books. Published three times a year.
Manuscripts to: R Smith, University of Durham.
Journal of Teacher Development
Pitman. Published quarterly.
Manuscripts to: M Golby, School of Education, University of Exeter.
The Leadership Quarterly: An International Journal of Political, Social and Behavioral Science
JAI Press. Published quarterly.
Manuscripts to: F Yammarino, State University of New York, USA.

Learning Resources Journal
    Learning Resources Development Group. Published three times a year.
    Manuscripts to: D Bosworth, Malford Grove, Gilvern, Abergavenny, Gwent.
Learning and Individual Differences: A Multidisciplinary Journal of Education
    JAI Press. Published quarterly.
    Manuscripts to: FN Dempster, University of Nevada, Las Vegas, USA, or
    F Yammarino, State University of New York, USA.
Management in Education
    Pitman. Published quarterly.
    Manuscripts to: The Editor, Putteridge Bury, University of Luton.
Medical Teacher
    Carfax. Published quarterly.
    Manuscripts to: RM Harden, Ninewells Hospital and Medical School.
Mentoring and Tutoring for Partnership in Learning
    Trentham Books. Published three times a year.
    Manuscripts to: J Egglestone, c/o Trentham Books, Stoke on Trent.
Multicultural Teaching to Combat Racism in School and Community
    Trentham Books. Published three times a year.
    Manuscripts to: G Klein, Department of Education, University of Warwick.
Pastoral Care in Education
    Blackwells. Published six times a year.
    Manuscripts to: R Best, Froebel Institute College, London.
Physics Education
    Institute of Physics Publishing. Published three times a year.
    Manuscripts to: Institute of Physics, Bristol.
Research in Drama Education
    Carfax. Published quarterly.
    Manuscripts to: J Somers, University of Exeter.
Research into Science and Technological Education
    Carfax, Twice a year.
    Manuscripts to: CR Brown, University of Hull.
Sport, Education and Society
    Carfax. Published quarterly.
    Manuscripts to: C Hardy, University of Loughborough.
Studies in the Education of Adults
    National Institution of Adult and Continuing Education. Published twice a year.
    Manuscripts to: J Wallis, Department of Educational Studies, University of Nottingham.
Teaching and Teacher Education
    Pergamon Press. Published six times a year.
    Manuscripts to: N. Bennett, University of Exeter.
Tertiary Education and Management
    Jessica Kingsley. Published twice a year.
    Manuscripts to: NR Begg, The University of Aberdeen.

Annotated Reading List

American Psychological Association (1983) *Publication Manual of the American Psychological Association*, 3rd edn, Washington, DC: American Psychological Association.
    A guide to the style for formal research papers required by a number of international journals.
Cave, R and Cave, J (1985) *Writing for Promotion and Profit: A guide to educational publishing*, Newmarket: Ron and Joyce Cave Educational Consultants.
    A short, rather oversimplified manual that concentrates on facts rather than skills and

provides some useful tips on getting published. It may help you to understand the contract, once you receive it.

Berry, R (1986) *How to Write a Research Paper*, Oxford: Pergamon.
A short book that covers a number of technical aspects, such as preparing a bibliography and dealing with footnotes, that I have not had space to cover in this chapter. Worth reading if you are new to publishing and lack a source of expert advice.

Open University Press (1993) *An Equal Opportunities Guide to Language and Image*, Buckingham: Open University Press.
Many publishers have guides to inclusive language. If yours does not, it is essential that you are aware of the hidden messages that your use of language may convey. The Open University Press guide is very short (19 pages), simple and user-friendly.

Collected Original Sources in Education: Carfax.
A microfiche journal dealing with original international educational research in full.

The following journals, all from Carfax, provide summaries of many hundred journal articles and/or books published across the world each year. They are a useful means of identifying the most up-to-date research and debate in particular areas of enquiry within education.

Content Pages in Education
Educational Technology
Higher Education Abstracts
Multicultural Education Abstracts
Research into Higher Education Abstracts
Sociology of Education Abstracts
Special Educational Needs Abstracts
Technical Education and Training Abstracts.

Index